EXCUSE ME WHILE I
SLIP INTO SOMEONE
MORE COMFORTABLE

ALSO BY ERIC POOLE

Where's My Wand?: One Boy's Magical Triumph over Alienation and Shag Carpeting

EXCUSE ME WHILE I SLIP INTO SOMEONE MORE COMFORTABLE

A MEMOIR

Eric Poole

· · · · · · · · · · ·

ROSETTABOOKS   NEW YORK

First edition published 2018 by RosettaBooks

Cover design by Christian Fuenfhausen
Interior design by Christian Fuenfhausen
Author photo by Chris Burbach

Library of Congress Control Number: 2017951388
ISBN-13 (print): 978-1-9481-2204-7
ISBN-13 (epub): 978-1-9481-2203-0

www.RosettaBooks.com
Printed in the United States of America

RosettaBooks®

For my mother, father, and sister, who watched me
make mistake after mistake, and loved me enough
to keep their mouths shut.

For my friends, who were in on the mistakes.

And for Sandy, who has been at my side for sixteen years
and still doesn't think it was a mistake.

CONTENTS

Many names and identifying characteristics have been changed to keep me from getting sued or yelled at in public. A few minor characters are composites to save having to introduce you to the countless number of people who flow in and out of one's life. And some sequences and details of events will doubtless be recalled differently by others who were (imagine this) comfortable in their own skin at the time and thus, perhaps, better able to assess the situations. What has not and could not be changed is my awkward, ridiculous journey of self-delusion and self-discovery. That part's exactly, 100 percent correct.

Chapter 1

MANILOW OF THE HOUR

The marching band of Hazelwood Central Senior High in St. Louis, Missouri, of which I was a member, was planning a hush-hush, invitation-only party hosted by Laurie Klingon, a popular flute player whose last name assured a lifetime of hilarious jokes at the hands of strangers.

And I had not been invited.

An out-of-town friend of Laurie's parents had thoughtfully died, thus creating a vacuum of parental supervision for the weekend. Word of the secret party naturally swept through the band, since it would have been pointless to exclude people if they didn't know about it.

"People are gonna talk about this party," Laurie announced to the select group as they stood in a corner of the football field casting faux-sympathetic looks at the rest of us, who were currently wishing them dead, "for years to come."

I had never been to a party that was not church related, a

venue where the attendees had to be nice to one another or God would cast everyone into hell. And that dearth of outside social experience gave this band party even more allure, filled as it was with people I admired. People I desperately wanted to befriend. People who were, in many cases, much better than me.

True, I *was* a minor celebrity in the Stage Band, known for my improvisational jazz trumpet solos (a mysterious ability, frankly, since no one else in our family had any musical aptitude whatsoever, and one that led me to frequently question whether I had been switched at birth, which would explain a lot of things). Dozens of students across the school were now vaguely aware of me. But the respect accorded my trumpet abilities had not led to new friendships or any real elevation in my status, inside or outside band.

And to further complicate matters, I was approaching six feet, two inches tall. I weighed in at a Dachau-fabulous 138 pounds. My wavy helmet hair made me look like a flapper who'd lost her cocaine. And of the two ears positioned astride my skull, only one operated, making it sometimes difficult to overhear the snide opinions being proffered by my schoolmates, which would have been a blessing had my imagination not constructed ones far worse.

Thus, I saw no reason why any party thrower would choose to invite me over any number of more handsome, feathered-haired, two-eared guys in band.

And as was obvious from the group standing in the corner of the football field, only the supercool members had been included—with the exception of my friend Mitch McKirby, a beak-nosed boy who was so blithely unaware of what other people thought that he played the clarinet. But Mitch's parents were good friends with Laurie's, and including him was obviously considered the price tag for silence.

Mitch was my ace in the hole. I began campaigning to be his plus-one.

"Think how much fun it would be to have me along," I said as we walked home from school that afternoon. "We could be like Starsky and Hutch, taking down the bad girls." I aimed my trumpet case like a gun, although in execution I appeared to be slightly more *Police Woman* than *Starsky and Hutch*.

"That doesn't make any sense," Mitch replied. "We both have brown hair." He switched his clarinet case to his other hand. "And why's it such a big deal, anyway? It's just a party."

Just a party, I thought. Just another nail in the coffin of my insignificance.

Suddenly, I was struck by a thought. Everyone knew that Mitch was, to put it mildly, the thrifty type.

"Tell you what," I proposed. "I'll buy your sloe gin. That's a savings of *three dollars*."

Word on the street was that, at this exclusive event, booze was being served—yet another reason the invitations were so coveted. Naturally, at age sixteen, I had never had a drink. My exposure to alcohol had been limited to the gasoline-flavored wines my parents drank as a celebration of the blood of Jesus, whose blood was now being shed most Saturday nights. And since Mother and Dad kept the liquor cabinet under lock and key, its allure had increased exponentially.

That did the trick.

"Okay," Mitch relented, "but don't embarrass me."

I was initially elated. But as the day of the party crept

closer, and I contemplated the very real fact that I had not been considered cool enough to be invited on my own, I realized that I would somehow need to re-create myself in the eyes of the band's elite. To become new and different. To sparkle.

And then, as if by divine inspiration, it came to me.

• • •

In 1977, Barry Manilow was pop's reigning king. He was, I decided, the perfect image in which to remake myself. After all, I had musical talent, just like Barry. And Barry had songs that made the girls swoon—songs *I* could play by ear to induce such swoons for myself. What girl wouldn't want to hear "It's a Miracle" on the trumpet?

Step, step, hip swivel, finger-gun cock.

I repeated this move over and over, alone in the family room of our suburban tract home, as I attempted to create a viable, supersexy strut that would emphasize my new pop star charisma while Manilow's "Jump Shout Boogie" shook the rafters.

Step, step, hip swivel, pause, and wink.

I held my trumpet casually in my right hand as the crowd of invisible adoring girls swooned.

Step, step, hip swivel, finger-gun—

"Oh, my God, WHAT are you doing?"

My nineteen-year-old sister Valerie stood staring at me, reeking of French fries, fresh from a stint chipping lard into a vat at the Cross Keys McDonald's.

Mortified, I switched off the stereo. "Nothing *you'd* understand."

"Obviously." She pulled off her name tag and threw it on the couch. "'Course, there's so much about you I don't understand."

"That's because you're not destined for stardom the way some of us are," I replied, trying to convince myself as much as her. "I'm becoming a commodity, so I have to work on my public persona."

"A commodity, huh?" She ambled down the hall to her bedroom. "Who on earth would wanna buy *you*?"

• • •

I spent the remaining couple of days before the party working on what I hoped was a brilliantly conceived ballad version of "Bandstand Boogie" and shopping for a pair of jeans that positively screamed studliness.

Finally, the big night arrived.

"Can I take your car?" I yelled into the laundry chute, the intercom to our mother's basement lair, the laundry room, where she spent most of her evenings bent over the ironing board ironing dish towels, sheets and place mats, and muttering colorful epithets about the lazy slobs upstairs who didn't share her exemplary work ethic.

A committed clean freak, she gave vivid and lustrous life to the term *obsessive-compulsive*, and my sister Val and I privately referred to her as General Patton in Pedal Pushers.

"Take it where?" Mother yelled back.

"To Laurie Klingon's house. We're having a band rehearsal there."

An important pop star accessory was a set of supercool wheels, and Mother's yellow Pontiac Firebird fit the bill perfectly. It was an automobile so ultra-hot that I was certain girls would want to pile into it like a clown car. Mitch, who lived down the street, had volunteered to drive us to the party, but his ride was a Plymouth Scamp, a car so boring that it almost begged to be punched.

"Who's Laurie Klingon?" Mother demanded.

"A flute player," I hollered. "Her dad's an orthodontist," I added, knowing that his lofty profession would resonate with Mother and Dad. Nothing bad could happen at the house of an almost doctor.

"Ray!" Mother yelled. "Put the Hoover by the garage door!" Any use of Mother's car required an immediate postmortem vacuuming of the rubber floor mats, no matter how late I returned it.

"Thanks!" I yelled, rolling my eyes.

I'm never gonna be like her, I thought as I flossed my teeth for the third time in preparation for my departure.

"Don't worry about dusting it," Dad whispered, letting me off the hook on wiping down the exterior surface of the car. "I'll wash it in the morning before she gets up." This was particularly kind of him, given that Mother only slept four hours a night and rose at 5:00 a.m., so Dad would have to wash the car in the dark.

He was an absurdly easygoing man who unfortunately acceded to Mother's every whim, having obviously decided that the only way to keep from blowing his head off was to go along with alphabetizing the Christmas decorations and waxing the driveway.

I thanked him as I grabbed a quart of orange juice from the refrigerator and headed for the car.

"Why are you taking the Minute Maid?" Dad asked.

"Oh," I replied airily, having anticipated this moment and rehearsed accordingly, "Laurie's just getting over scurvy."

• • •

As my friend Mitch and I pulled up to Laurie's house in the yellow hottiemobile, I was disappointed to see only two people witnessing our arrival. Bonnie Parkin—a formerly chunky girl who had recently lost sixty pounds—sidled up to the car.

"Hey, Eric," she purred, "nice car. I might want to make out on it."

"God, Bonnie," Leslie Brockmeyer whispered, "reel it in."

Leslie—who talked in a voice so soft that people were constantly banging the sides of their heads and screaming, "What?!"—was a pretty blonde who had been Bonnie's best friend until Bonnie had had the audacity to lose weight.

"I'll take a rain check!" I replied in what I hoped was a sexy, he-devil voice, alternately pleased to be singled out and bummed that more people weren't around to see it.

"I didn't mean with *you*," she replied.

I slunk into the house. The party was in full swing. Donna Summer blared from the stereo. Carrying my trumpet case in anticipation of noodling a few refrains to impress the ladies, along with the orange juice that Laurie had instructed Mitch to bring, I tentatively auditioned my new swagger.

Step, step, hip swivel, wink.

I scanned the living room, hoping to note some random fainting. No one appeared to have even noticed. Guys and girls tripped over one another, spilling booze on the beige shag carpeting and laughing loudly. I couldn't wait to join them.

"This is friggin' great," said Tommy Sedgwick, a tuba player who could have been mistaken for a *Tiger Beat* pinup, as he held up his plastic cup. He was blond, Nordic looking, and very confident, and I had often fantasized what it would be like to be with him.

To *be* him.

Girls flocked to him like he was a teen idol, which was particularly annoying, since he had no talent and played a stupid instrument. He had his arm around Kathy Kennemeyer, a pretty brunette who was shy but very sweet.

Tommy handed Kathy his cup as he turned his attentions to a buxom blonde. "Go get me another one."

I smiled at Kathy and shrugged as if to say, "What are you gonna do? He's our John Travolta."

I pushed Mitch through the living room, eager to find Laurie and claim our share of the illicit liquor, but he kept trailing behind, staring at the already tipsy band members as though he were on safari. At any moment I expected him to whip out a Super 8 camera or toss them raw meat.

We spotted Laurie seated in the dining room, which she had turned into a corner liquor store. Laurie had, as she would mysteriously intone, "connections"—which we presumed to be mob ties but which was actually just a loser brother who would buy her booze for a price—and she sat next to two cartons of pint-size bottles of sloe gin. I stepped back to allow Mitch to go first.

"Hey, Laurie," he said, giving her the Mr. Spock hand greeting that she had become resigned to.

"Great party!" I piped up.

"What's *he* doing here?" she said to Mitch.

I blanched, horrified to be considered a crasher. I assumed Mitch had gotten her blessing. He just shrugged, obviously aware that he held all the cards when it came to keeping this blowout quiet.

"Pay her," he said to me.

She pulled out two bottles of sloe gin. "That'll be ten dollars."

My relief at her apparent forgiveness was somewhat dampened by the fact that she was ripping me off. She had told the invitees earlier in the week that these bottles cost *three* dollars. Apparently, there was a four-dollar gate-crashing fee.

But I had seen what alcohol did for my parents. As upstanding Baptists, Mother and Dad were careful not to get drunk, lest they blow their biblical rationale for knocking back a few. But even one or two drinks appeared to have magical effects. After a bottle of Mateus, the squat, clay-bottled wine, Mother would mysteriously transform into a sort of Carol Brady—relaxed, charming, and most remarkably, maternal. And Dad became his own man, a confident, suburban version of Dirty Harry.

This booze, I knew, could help me step into my new self. Especially since I no longer had the mystical help of Endora.

At the age of eight, I had developed a firm and intractable belief in magic. This had sprung from a desire to escape the traumatic world around me and had manifested as attempts to replicate the on-screen magic of Endora from the TV series *Bewitched*.

This magic had helped me to cope with a mother whose cataclysmic mood swings were outshone only by her mania for perfection; a school life rich with bullies, intimidation, and an impressive dearth of friends; the sudden, inexplicable deaths of people I loved; and the torture that can only come from having a physical defect. Magic had been my saving grace.

But now that I had matured to a fully realized adult of sixteen, I had come to understand that magic—more than some sort of otherworldly power—came from within. That believing in myself was the real, true magic.

I paid the ten dollars.

"You do know," Laurie said snidely, noting the trumpet case I was carrying, "that we have a stereo, right?" She leaned closer and hollered, "Can you hear it?"

• • •

"If you drink it through a straw, it'll hit you faster."
"What?"

Leslie Brockmeyer repeated herself at a slightly louder whisper as we all leaned in. We had no idea if this was true or not, but at this point it was moot, since most of us had consumed half a pint of sloe gin each and were pretty much tanked.

"Oh, that's *all* you need," Mitch—who, after tasting the sloe gin, had elected to abstain from alcohol consumption—yelled over the music, as he looked up from a Time/Life Civil War book he was reading.

The judgment implicit in his remark was lost on me. I was far too busy experiencing physical and emotional sensations unlike anything I had ever known. I felt flushed and giddy and packed with personality.

Mother and Dad's religious commitment to moderation suddenly seemed absurd. Surely God wouldn't get his panties in a wad about this. It seemed to provide nothing but positive effects. Heck, I thought, why can't I drink everywhere that I'm uncomfortable—in gym class, during family dinners, at church?

Even though the people I counted as friends numbered only a handful of the band's eighty members, and even fewer of the thirty or so who were at the party, I now found myself almost eager to embrace the spotlight. Only two hours had passed, but I was flirting with girls so far outside my league they could have been playing another sport.

I think I might be rockin' this party, I said to myself. *Maybe I should get my trumpet out.*

Bonnie stumbled by, her motor skills obviously on the fritz. I performed an abbreviated version of my Barry strut, careful not to overdo it lest I drive her insane with desire. She stopped and looked me up and down as she wobbled in place, her eyes now slightly crossed. "Nice jeans."

"Thanks."

"They make your butt look good." She slapped me playfully on the behind.

"Your shirt is really flattering, too," I replied. "That pink goes great with your bloodshot eyes."

Leslie overheard and laughed uproariously, a nearly audible *tee-hee* escaping her lips. Mitch sighed heavily and looked at his watch.

Bonnie leaned in close, nearly toppling over. "You're a bad boy. I should spank you for that."

"Oh, yeah?" I replied. "You're all talk and no do."

She took my hand to lead me toward a closet.

Suddenly, I began to panic. What was she gonna do to me?

What would I be expected to do to her? Exactly how did all this stuff work? I was pretty good at making out, having been taught by Wendy Hollister from church, who told me, "You kiss nice. Like a girl." But the rest of it was still something of a mystery.

Bonnie was reaching for the doorknob when we were interrupted by Tommy.

"Hey, I've got an idea," he yelled to the assembled partygoers. "Let's TP Mark Danson's house!"

"Yeah!" I hollered quickly, mopping the ocean of sweat that had formed on my brow.

A cheer went up from the assembled group. Mark, who was out of town with his parents, was a beloved member of the band. Both approachable to the girls and nonthreatening to the boys, Mark was the funniest guy we knew, and thus it made perfect sense to demonstrate that affection by heaving rolls of toilet paper into his front yard.

Although typically loath to break rules of any sort—at age eleven, I had spent months evading the cops after removing the tag on my bedroom mattress—tonight was different. Tonight, I was a risk taker.

A plan of attack was immediately mapped out. Several kids ran to the Schnucks supermarket to buy the goods, while the other thirty of us coordinated carpools.

"I don't think this is a very good idea," Mitch, now the party's official pooper, declared loudly, to virtually no one's consternation. He turned to Laurie, who was atop the coffee table attempting to do the Hustle. "I should just stay here."

"Yes, you should," Laurie replied, "but nobody stays without me, and I'm goin'." She teetered off the coffee table and hit the floor, one of her cork wedges flying off.

The suburban streets were fairly deserted at 11:00 p.m., and everyone made it the two miles to Mark's house intact, an enormous blessing we cheerfully took for granted. We parked our cars a block away and noisily crept up to the house, loaded down with armfuls of toilet paper.

On Tommy's "Go!" we began frantically unspooling the rolls and hurling them into the giant oak tree in the front yard. Long curls of white paper began to drape the tree. As one of the tallest kids, I aimed for the highest branches, and found to my delight—and the unbecoming amazement of my bandmates—that my drunken pitches were better than my sober ones in gym class.

Kathy Kennemeyer, who was standing near me, mimed applause as I took a bow after each successful attempt. Exhilaration coursed through my body—*Kathy thinks I'm a jock!* I sneaked a glance at her. She looked like a Kewpie doll—bee-stung lips, porcelain skin, and the sweetest smile I had ever seen. She caught me staring and laughed as though we were sharing a private joke.

I directed her to help me wrap the fir trees that ringed the yard. As we circled the trees, enrobing them in paper, I attempted to run as coolly as possible, incorporating my patented *step, step, hip swivel* into my gait as best I could.

"Oh," Kathy said, clucking her tongue sympathetically. "Do you have hip dysplasia? I knew a kid in grade school who had that."

The group was almost finished, thousands of yards of toilet paper turning the lawn into either a magical winter wonderland or a giant outhouse, depending on how drunk you were, when we heard the sirens.

"Run!" Tommy screamed.

Panicked, we dropped the remaining rolls and scattered like roaches, scurrying for our cars as the police roared up. Mitch and I jumped into the Firebird as the cops hemmed in several other people's cars. Kathy stood frozen on the sidewalk, unsure what to do.

I threw my car door open. "Get in!"

She dove into the backseat and I took off before the door was even closed, nearly sideswiping an orange Pinto as we screeched down the street.

"Ohmigodohmigod, did they get your license plate?" Mitch cried, breathing heavily. "Oh, we're gonna be in so much trouble!"

"I don't know if they did or not," I replied, trying to keep my bleary focus on the road. "Kathy, did you see anything?"

"I think they were too busy rounding people up," Kathy responded from the backseat.

"Ohmigod, they're gonna come arrest us at home!" Mitch shrieked. "I hope you're proud of yourselves. I didn't even want to be a part of this! Now I'm gonna have a criminal record!"

I glanced at myself in the rearview mirror. In my gloriously inebriated state, even the thought of Mother having to bail me out of jail didn't scare me.

Too much.

"I think they got Tommy," Kathy said quietly. "Wow. He's gonna be a felon." She reached out and touched my arm. "Thanks for saving me."

I smiled. As I drove, miraculously managing to avoid hitting the cars parked on either side of the wide street, a series of images began to play across my mind: Kathy and I cruising through the school parking lot in the Firebird, holding hands and waving to those in lesser cars; making a formal announcement to the marching band that we were going steady; being crowned homecoming king and queen and getting married in the ballroom of the glamorous Tan-Tar-A Resort at Lake of the Ozarks, where I played "Looks Like We Made It" on my trumpet as Kathy came down the aisle. I hoped our marriage would last longer than Barry's did.

"Watch out!" Kathy suddenly yelled, yanking me out of my reverie. I swerved to avoid taking out a garden gnome mailbox.

"Okay, that's it," Mitch snapped. "Pull over. You're weaving around like Dorothy Hamill."

At Mitch's house, he climbed out of the driver's seat and turned to Kathy and me. "If I get nabbed, you're going down with me," he promised, slamming the door and stalking up the driveway.

I sighed and looked at Kathy. "Do you want me to take you home?"

"No," she replied. "I should probably go to Laurie's first."

Sobered by the near miss, I drove carefully back to the Klingon house. Only a quarter of the kids had returned. I was expecting a debriefing and lots of "wow, how close was that?" chatter, but there appeared to be very little talking going on. The lights had been turned down low, and several guys were clumsily attempting to get to second base as their girlfriends feigned the requisite disapproval. Bonnie had traipsed into a closet with a trombone player and all we could hear were weird slurping sounds. In an irony lost on those present, strains of the Commodores' "Easy" wafted from the Magnavox stereo.

Laurie passed out half-drunk bottles of sloe gin. "A toast," she announced. "To our fallen comrades." We all raised our pint bottles in salute and downed a slug. "Okay," she continued. "Who wants to play spin the sloe gin?"

Everybody enthusiastically gathered around as Laurie explained the rules. A bottle would be spun. Whoever it stopped on would have to turn and kiss the person on their left, or drink the entire remaining contents of that bottle.

"Make a big circle."

I was standing two people down from John Runyon, a good-looking drummer who had a great smile and confidence to burn, and with whom I had become sometime friends, since he lived around the corner and we shared a passion for music. I instinctively moved down to stand on his left, since, obviously, it's more fun to play games next to someone you know.

John turned to me. "It should be boy-girl, not boy-boy," he said loudly, pointing to a space between Kathy and Leslie Brockmeyer. Several people snickered as I turned beet red and slunk over, rolling my eyes to cover my embarrassment. I just wasn't *thinking*.

John spun the bottle. It landed on Kathy.

"Oooohhh…" the crowd responded with anticipation.

I was on her left. She turned to me and smiled apologetically. "Um, well, since I think I'm gonna be dating Tommy…"

"Does he know that?" Laurie sniped. Meow.

Kathy picked up the bottle.

"Chug! Chug!"

She gulped the contents heroically. As everyone applauded, she grabbed a new bottle, placed it in the middle of the circle and spun. The bottle's neck slowed to a stop in front of me. I turned to Leslie, who was on my left, assuming what I hoped was my studliest guise.

"Chug! Chug!" she began, leading the world's first whispered drinking cheer.

Fortunately, this rejection was assuaged by the fact that I was really quite drunk and, as I poured the couple ounces of additional alcohol down my gullet, getting drunker fast. So drunk that I barely noticed as couples slowly began to break off from the game.

A stalwart six of us hung in there, less out of a desire to keep the game going than because we were simply too loaded to get up. I gazed blearily around at the group and realized something profound: these people, many of whom I even knew by name, were my closest and dearest friends, and always would be.

And then I passed out.

●　●　●

I was awakened a half hour later by the sounds of Laurie and John, who were sucking face with such ferocity that I feared one of them would lose a lung.

I pulled myself up, and staggered down the hall to get my coat and trumpet. I had yet to premiere any Manilow music, I realized. As I veered into the bedroom where the coats had been stacked, I spotted Kathy lying on the bed, alone, sniffling.

I stopped suddenly, unsure whether to get my stuff or just leave. "You okay?"

She didn't look at me. "I'm fine. It's... nothing."

"Doesn't sound like nothing."

I tried to swagger across the room to sit down on the bed. *I will soothe her*, I thought to myself. *I will be her Dreamweaver.*

Equilibrium issues, however, along with the focus required to conclude my strut with a finger-gun cock, caused a synapse short circuit, and as I missed the edge of the bed and collapsed onto the floor in a heap of Brittania patchwork jeans and Givenchy cologne, Kathy bolted upright.

"Are *you* okay?"

"Fine, fine," I replied quickly, scrambling to my feet. "Sooooo… do you want to talk about it?"

"I don't know," she said hesitantly, then, with barely a pause, blurted out, "It's Tommy. He keeps flirting with me, but he never asks me out."

"Yeah, I know," I responded as I took aim at the bed once again, this time with success.

"And I shouldn't really care. It's just, *he's so cute.*"

Amen, I said to myself, noting that I was merely appreciating him in the spiritual manner in which God appreciates all his children. "But you deserve better."

"Thanks."

"You deserve a guy who will play Barry Manilow songs for you and buy you a mood ring and get *you* another sloe gin and orange juice." I paused. "You want another sloe gin and orange juice?"

"No, that's okay." She gazed at me and smiled. "You're really sweet, you know that?"

I reached down and pulled my trumpet out of the case.

"What are you doing?"

Without a word, I launched into a chorus of "Tryin' to Get the Feeling Again."

She gave me a funny look, as though she were somehow seeing me for the first time, and then suddenly, without warning, she leaned forward, pushed the trumpet away from my face, and kissed me.

Slowly, delicately, her tongue began to explore my mouth. She fell back on the bed, pulling my body on top of her. My mind raced. What exactly was I supposed to do next? What would Barry do?

Oh, right. Fourplay.

Darren Pulaski—a fellow Royal Ambassador at our church who, for years, had counseled me on matters of sex, religion, and his favorite subject, "stealing shit from the Quick Shop"—had told me about this fourplay business, although I wasn't entirely clear what the number four had to do with it.

I reached under her shirt to unhook her bra. I couldn't figure out how the clasp worked, and after several minutes of fumbling and *Wait, I think I've got it*s, Kathy reached back, and with one swift move unhooked and slipped off her shirt and bra.

Wow... interesting, I thought as I surveyed the female landscape before me. I grasped one of her breasts and twisted it intently, as though opening a jar of mayonnaise.

"Ow!" she protested.

She gently pulled my head down and planted my mouth on her other breast. This felt kind of good. I found myself getting more and more excited as I began to grind my body against hers, although given that my head was at chest level, I was mostly humping her leg.

Please God, I prayed, *tomorrow, let Kathy tell everyone what an expert lover I am.* Let this news seal my rep as a rock star, so that the band's coolest members beg to ride shotgun in the Firebird. Let it drive those weird feelings for Tommy Sedgwick and John Runyon from my head.

Suddenly, it occurred to me. There was one surefire way to ensure that I buried those feelings right alongside the old lackluster Eric.

I must touch her bad spot.

This was, of course, an extremely risky proposition. I had always been an upstanding Baptist, having served as a Royal Ambassador (the holy version of Boy Scouts), where I judged the morally bankrupt actions of other sinners with swift and impressive condemnation.

In fact, I had been supportive of Mother and Dad's decision to withdraw from the church we had long attended because it wasn't conservative *enough*—more, perhaps, because it meant not having to attend services three times a week than for any particular religious stance, but still.

I even supported their decision to begin blasting the taped sermons of Reverend B. R. Tibbits throughout the house. B. R. was a southern minister whose militaristic analyses of biblical texts offered a multitude of reasons why God should strike pretty much everyone dead. His sermons—conveniently offered on reel-to-reel tapes—now lined the walls of our rathskeller, alphabetically arranged according to sin.

So how, as a good Christian, could I rationalize spiritually devastating out-of-wedlock sex?

I mentally raced over the landscape of possibilities. Given my musical talent and how well this new persona was going, surely God wanted me to become an actual superstar. So perhaps, I thought, as I yanked my Brittanias down, squirming and thrashing to push them past my knees, God made dispensation for such acts by those he deemed worthy, when done in the pursuit of the stardom he had decreed.

Kathy gently slid her pants off, and, with my jeans hovering around my shins, I began to manually probe her honey pot with all the delicacy and finesse of a butcher cleaning out a turkey.

The sensation was odd. It reminded me of the Halloween haunted houses where, in total darkness, someone would stick my hand in a bowl of spaghetti and I would scream like a girl. Fortunately, this time I didn't.

She began to kiss me with more urgency, fueling my courage. I was now a man on a mission. In my sexiest, drunken, platinum recording artist–style voice I sang, "This one's fffor you," as I attempted to masterfully jam my ding-a-ling into her.

"Ow!" she cried. "Slow down."

Mortified, I stopped. "Ssssorry," I slurred. "Should I, um?"

She took a deep breath and, as she exhaled, said, "Okay. Now."

As I entered her, I could feel the same ecstatic feeling rising in me that occurred whenever I touched myself while watching Alex Trebek on *High Rollers*. My body, my mind, my soul were filled with a potent blend of rock star machismo and Baptist fear.

I began to thrust with rapturous abandon and wild ineptness for what felt like many seconds as a feeling of uncontrollable bliss built inside me. Then, as I neared the moment of nirvana, another uncontrollable feeling began to develop—one so vast, so consuming, and so immediate that I had no warning.

I pulled out of her and vainly tried to scoot to the foot of the bed, my head making it only as far as her hips, before I vomited.

Onto her vagina.

• • •

Perhaps unsurprisingly, few words were exchanged between us after that. Kathy leaped out of bed and rushed into the bathroom, screaming and whimpering, and after several hastily mumbled *I'm sorrys*, I stumbled out the door wishing I were both dead and the real Barry Manilow. Anyone but me.

Even after I purged the last round of liquor from my stomach in the grass by Laurie's driveway, no cop would have required a Breathalyzer to arrest me. Fortunately, I encountered none on the quiet suburban streets as I drove home at twenty miles an hour, trying to remember where it was I lived. After missing the turn onto my street several times since there appeared to be new, multiple lanes (which were actually the Hormans' front lawn), I finally managed the difficult curving right onto Woodpath Drive.

As I weaved down the street, I somehow grasped that making the turn into our driveway would be far too precarious. As I reached the house, I made an executive decision and simply stopped the car in the middle of the street, proudly noting, as I staggered up the driveway to the front door, that I had had the presence of mind to turn the car off.

I held up mother's key ring next to the porch light, attempting to decipher which key worked the front door, unswayed by the label that read "house." I inserted a random key into the lock. Then another. Then another.

Well, this is just ridiculous, I thought to myself. *I could be here all night, and I really need to get some shut-eye.* I leaned against the door and began ringing the doorbell continuously.

After what felt like hours but was perhaps thirty seconds, my father opened the door. Since I had been leaning on it,

I fell into the foyer. He stood over my crumpled heap for a moment, then took the keys from me and said firmly, "We'll talk about this tomorrow."

• • •

I awoke the next morning feeling wildly under the weather. My head pounded. Dried puke flaked the corners of my mouth. My neck was stiff. I opened my eyes to discover that I was lying on the floor of the bathroom, my head propped up against the wall.

Oh. My. God. The memory hit me like a brick. I threw up on Kathy's cootchie. Had Laurie heard? Would Kathy tell everyone? Would I ever live this down? Had I made God mad?

I pulled myself into a standing position. My brain seemed to be swimming inside my head, tilting first one way, then the other. As I opened the bathroom door, the bright morning light slapped me in the face. Squinting, nauseated, I shuffled in a turtle-like fashion across the hall to my bedroom.

I threw back the covers—without even folding them on a perfect diagonal—and collapsed onto the bed. Realizing the door was still open, I crawled heavily across the mattress to reach for it, just as Dad appeared in the doorway.

"Just curious," he said, with an edge in his voice that I rarely heard. "Where's your trumpet?"

Ugh. In all the hubbub, I must have forgotten it at Laurie's.

"I don't feel good," I replied, flopping back onto the bed and digging my face into the pillows.

"Oh, trust me," he replied, "you're gonna feel a whole lot worse when we get done with you."

As I lay there, my stomach roiling, my head pounding, I couldn't evade the truth: my attempt to redefine myself had not been quite the rousing success I had hoped. And I may have done spiritual damage to my soul in the process.

But it *had* helped me to impress a supercute girl. So maybe there was just some element missing—some aspect that I had not quite managed to embody. *Perhaps*, I thought, *if I can figure out what that is, I can carry this persona into the whole of my life.*

My mother appeared at the door, looking terribly concerned, which was an enormous relief and frankly, a shock. How wonderful, I thought, that she was more worried for my health and safety than the fact that I had erred.

She held up a glass.

"You want some orange juice?"

As I went flying into the bathroom, my hand over my mouth, I could almost swear I saw her laugh.

···· Chapter 2 ····

TRUTH OR DARE

"The Traveliers will be performing in the annual Winter Wonderland concert in the cafeteria tonight," Principal Nibley droned over the school PA in his patented What the Fuck Has Become of My Life tone. "They've got the music in them," he mumbled, the razor poised over his wrists, "so I know we'll all want to be there."

There was a slight pause. "Provided no one calls in a bomb threat."

This last part wasn't so much a warning as a helpful suggestion, since the principal was forced to attend these extracurricular extravaganzas.

"Oh, and congratulations to Eric Poole and Barbara Fassler," he added, almost as an afterthought, "who are nominees for"—there was a shuffle of papers—"the William Danforth *I Dare You* Award." This was followed by a muffled thump as he clamped his hand over the microphone and shouted, "Is this *right?*"

Alternately thrilled and shocked as I sat at my desk in first-period English, I wondered the same thing. Although I had always been a good student, scoring stellar grades in almost any subject that involved creativity, colorful dental hygiene, or a blow-up accident victim, I was not exactly known as the *daring* type.

Tony Tropler, for one, could attest to this. Tony was a high-ranking official in the burnout contingent—those weed-smoking members of the student body who were voted Most Likely to Require a Court-Appointed Lawyer—and he was my personal torturer.

"Hey, fairy, score any touchdowns lately?"

Tony was standing next to my locker, referencing a recent gym class where—exhilarated at having actually caught a football and panicked at what to do next—I charged down the field and scored a touchdown. For the opposing team.

I glanced around to see who had heard him, praying that the din of hallway chatter obscured his words.

"Yeah, that wasn't my best day," I said, forcing a smile. "But I guess when you're as creative as I am, you gotta sacrifice things like a sense of direction." I knocked on my head. "Only so much space up here!"

Tony was wearing a shirt that was unbuttoned almost to his navel, and his puka-shell necklace fairly glowed against his tanned skin. He moved closer, pinning me up against the locker, his necklace nearly serrating my flesh.

"If you ever do that again," he seethed, "I'll kill you."

Tony was frequently offering to snuff me out—a generous proposition, to be sure, since it meant getting blood on the puka shells and an unplanned sojourn in cellblock H if he left behind any evidence.

Sadly, he was but the latest in a series of hooligans who had added a special brand of bedlam to my days since grade school. It had all begun with Tim, a ginger (do the math—he had his own issues) at Brown Elementary, who had come up with the scintillating sobriquet "One-Ear"—which he routinely bellowed while attempting to perform a lobotomy on me with a dodge ball. From Tim, the succession of bottom feeders grew, eventually providing me with a constantly turning kaleidoscope of humiliation.

Tony, my latest—who was clearly vying for the appendage "and greatest"—specialized in a form of psychological warfare that set him apart from the random jerks who populated Hazelwood Central's bully brigade. He was more than happy to provide—while simply standing in the lunch line or the boys' locker room—disturbing and graphic details about the manner in which he planned to execute me.

I did not have the courage to be daring with Tony. The only place I had the courage to be daring was with music.

Like my hero, Barry Manilow, I both sang *and* played an instrument. My vocal talents were now on daily display in the concert choir. And my skills as a trumpet player—creating dazzling improvisational solos (albeit dazzling by dint of the fact that no one else in the trumpet section had any improvisational ability whatsoever)—were regularly showcased at our Stage Band concerts.

I secretly longed to join our glee club, the Travaliers, who performed contemporary music and who were clearly grooming America's next generation of pop stars. But my talents as a trumpeter necessitated a creative choice; I did not have the time to become a star at both. I would start with the trumpet, and hopefully, as Barry did, let my singing career blossom later.

Becoming a star was essential. For stardom meant elevation not only into the ranks of the cool kids in band, but of the entire Hazelwood Central elite. There, jocks and homecoming princesses alike would be vying for my attention, clawing at my bell-bottoms, desperate for a piece of the Poole. And stardom meant a loss of power over me from people like Tony Tropler.

"Do you ever wonder," I asked my friend Mitch one afternoon as we walked home from school (a journey accomplished by simply shimmying through the hole someone had dug underneath the fence that separated the high school from our backyards), "if you have a destiny?"

Mitch tossed me his clarinet case. "You mean, like Jesus?"

"Well, not so much the nailed-to-a-cross business," I replied, although my torture by Tony felt awfully crucifixion-like. "Just like you're meant to be, I don't know, famous or something."

"Famous?" He did the limbo under the chain link. "For what?"

I sighed. I was surrounded by people who seemed so content to be unknown. What was wrong with them? I had been nominated for the prestigious *I Dare You* Award, and in just two weeks our Stage Band was headed to the state finals, where I hoped to blow away the competition with a spectacular solo. These were the rewards of striving, of complete and utter dissatisfaction with one's life.

If my destiny is indeed stardom, I thought as Mitch and I headed for our respective houses, *preparations have to be made.* The white-hot glare of stardom had felled lesser men than I, and I needed to be absolutely ready for my moment in the spotlight. More than ever, it was clear that I needed to perfect the new Eric so that I could spring him on the world at large.

I began to redouble my efforts at celebrity transformation, spending hours at home alone incorporating other Barry Manilow traits that I felt would add to my celebrity luster. These included using his song titles and lyrics as conversational elements—a device that was, I felt, a brilliantly subliminal move that would reinforce my connection to musical superstardom and remind those within earshot of my escalating profile.

"Looks like we made it!" I announced to the trumpet section after a particularly good Stage Band rehearsal, covertly attempting to sing/speak the melody line of the Manilow song in question.

"Made what?" my fellow trumpet player Jim replied.

As was often the case, this left me with nowhere to go, since the next line of the song—"Left each other on the way to another love"—somehow seemed inappropriate when spoken to a group of men holding large brass baseball bats.

It was clear that I was not dealing with rocket scientists, so I decided to be a bit more direct going forward. I began rehearsing the entire Manilow catalog so that I could effortlessly noodle choruses of various hits on my trumpet during warm-ups.

"God, don't you know anybody else's songs?" Jim asked loudly.

It was third-period concert band, and my face turned crimson. This was not on my mentally approved list of compliments.

"I can't help it," I huffed, "that I can play by ear."

"Well, that doesn't mean that you should annoy the hell out of everyone with all that Barry Manilow crap," Jim snapped.

Crap?

Everything went black. Who thought Barry Manilow was crap? Sure, there were drummers who only got into Foreigner and Styx, and flautists who were all about Judas Priest, although no one really cared what flute players thought. Barry was middle-of-the-road, but he was superpopular.

I glanced around to see if others had heard him and were nodding their agreement, snickering at the deluded trumpet player who thought "Daybreak" was cool. But no one seemed to be paying any attention.

"Do you think Barry Manilow is over?" I asked Mitch tentatively on our walk home.

"That would be like saying," he declared indignantly as he threw me his clarinet case before shimmying under the fence, "that stamp collecting is for losers."

Perhaps Mitch wasn't the best judge, since he had been a philatelist as long as I had known him and was understandably touchy about it. Mitch's family had a thirty-foot-long aboveground pool, but for the neighborhood kids, even that draw could barely subsume the horror of being forced to hold a magnifying glass over the postal depictions of FDR and the Japanese beetle.

But his words made me feel better. Even if Mitch wasn't cool, he was kind. And he was the perfect friend: as a clarinetist, he was naturally lower on the band totem pole. And as a 5.5 (to my six) on the looks scale, Mitch didn't overshadow me in hotness, a crucial element given my deeply held fear that I was, essentially, an electric pole with acne.

"Barry Manilow," Mitch replied, "is a god."

"Thank you," I said, relieved. "If you want, I'll come over and look at stamps."

Perhaps I'm just trying too hard to draw a musical connection to my hero, I thought when I got home. Maybe my embodiment of Barry should be more about the body.

I decided to start with my hair. Carefully scotch-taping the album covers of *Tryin' to Get the Feeling* and *This One's for You* to the mirrored tiles in the bathroom, I began attempting to style my newly grown-out locks into a feathery bouffant, using the cover photos as a guide. With the help of my sister's sophisticated new nine-hundred-watt blow-dryer and a can of Aqua Net stolen from my mother, I was eventually able to create a decent approximation, with one small exception: Barry's locks were blond, and mine were a brown so boring it was typically found ejecting from the anuses of cows.

Then I remembered that my sister, Val, had been auditioning a new product called Sun-In, a magical hair lightener that required only some time in the sun or under a blow-dryer to turn your hair a dazzling shade of sun-kissed gold. Problem solved.

The next afternoon, while Mother and Dad were at work and Val was at school, I borrowed her Sun-In for a trial run.

The first application gave my hair a slight auburn tint. This was encouraging—I was on my way to rock star hair, although I would need to step things up and apply a bit more product.

One hour and an entire bottle of Sun-In later, I stood admiring my handiwork in the mirror, the blow-dryer still whirring like a jet engine in my hand. Although a tad stiff, and not quite the shade of Barry's, my hair was indeed now closer to blond than brunette.

I saw a flash of hip-huggers and nose as my sister sailed past. She stopped suddenly and backed up into the doorway, her mouth agape.

"Have you lost your *mind*?!"

Between college courses, her part-time job, and her boyfriend Bobby (a man so good-looking he never bothered to speak in complete sentences, correctly assuming that hot people should only open their mouths to accept compliments), Val was rarely home. But when she was, she had opinions.

"You aren't seriously gonna go out in public looking like Lucille Ball...?"

"It's not red, it's blond!" I yelled defensively. "Like Barry Manilow's!"

"Are you color-blind?" She reached up and broke off a strand of my hair, easily accomplished since it was now so damaged that it stuck almost straight out from my head. She handed it to me. "You look like you belong under the big top."

Mother and Dad's reactions were slightly less tactful.

"I told you to stay out of the Tarn-X!" Dad snapped.

"It's just hair lightener," I replied. "Everyone's doing it."

"Well," Mother said with a sigh as she dropped her purse on the kitchen table, "what's going on inside that head of yours is a complete mystery. But now the whole world can see what's going on *outside*."

As much as *I* liked my new strawberry blond–meets– Day-Glo orange hairdo, I was, I had to admit, a bit nervous about debuting it at school the next day. Ours was not an academic institution that welcomed dramatic transformations in its male students. And much as I longed for attention, giving Tony a fresh reason to attempt homicide seemed, at best, ill advised.

Add to this the fact that I had to apply a thin coat of Vaseline to the haystack on my head to give it any sort of manageability, and it was with a great deal of apprehension that I slunk into school the next morning, glancing around covertly as I attempted to gauge the responses of fellow students. Various kids whispered and pointed, their actions ambiguous and difficult to judge.

"Hey, fairy," Tony Tropler said as he sidled up to me, his actions less ambiguous and difficult to judge. "Halloween was last month."

I laughed, trying to turn his insult into a shared amusement. "Yeah, I know, crazy, huh? My sister got a little carried away. She said since I'm gonna be a star soon, I should look like one."

"You?" he snorted. "A star?"

"Well, you know," I replied tentatively, afraid to contradict him, "with the Stage Band stuff, and this award nomination and all."

"The only award you're gonna win," he said loudly, flicking my hair with his middle finger, "is for best impersonation of a fag." He high-fived Joe, one of the made men who always stood behind him like talent-free Pips.

I'll show him, I thought to myself as the bell mercifully rang. I turned to rush into my first-period English class, but Tony tripped me, and I stumbled across the hallway, making a less-than-starlike entrance into the classroom, where various kids looked up at me, wide-eyed. I sat down next to my bandmate Shelly, still hyperventilating. Shelly was a sweet, supportive girl whose short hair was the color of filthy dishwater, and I hoped that at least *she* was capable of seeing the celebrity sparkle in this new look.

She gazed at me and leaned over. I tried to shake off the hallway humiliation as I tilted my good ear toward her.

"You know," she whispered, "you might wanna rethink that."

I slumped down in my chair as our teacher, Mrs. Campbell, stood up from behind her desk.

"Good morning, everyone."

The class quickly quieted. Few teachers were accorded the fear and respect Mrs. Campbell was. A no-nonsense woman who possessed a marked distaste for the superficiality of beauty regimens, Mrs. Campbell favored utilitarianism in both her hairstyles and clothes, a quality that did her lackluster features no favors. She wore the bare minimum of make-up—a slash of nude lipstick and, occasionally, some mascara to remind us that she didn't moonlight as a prison guard on weekends. But she loved literature and did her damnedest to pass that love along to her motley group of first-period students, most of whom were far too crusty-eyed to even spell their names correctly at 7:30 a.m.

Unfortunately, she also had an uncanny ability to read the faces of her pupils, calling on whoever was either most unprepared or about to lose consciousness, and she seemed to delight in the mortification that came from being roused from a dead sleep with a question about Orwell or Dostoyevsky.

"I know how much you all enjoy reading," she barked. A gasp of panic arose from those awake enough to comprehend. "So, for next Friday, I'd like you to read and do a book report on John Steinbeck's *The Grapes of Wrath*."

Murmurs of grief and despair surged through the class. I actually adored reading—I had read hundreds of books and was currently on an Art Buchwald bender—but like the rest of the class, I moaned and put my head in my hands. A week after this was due, we were headed to the state Stage Band competition, and I had much Manil-izing and many hours of trumpet practice to get in. This competition could be the beginning of my new life.

Mrs. Campbell walked around her desk and down the left-hand aisle, stopping between Shelly and me. She had an understandably surprised look as she stared down at my distraught expression. After band, English was my best and favorite subject, and I'd always tried to curry favor with Mrs. C, a fact of which she was well aware.

"I'm sorry, Mr. Poole," she said, staring down at me, "does this book report interfere with your busy schedule of hair processing?" Half the class erupted in titters, a reaction that I desperately hoped had less to do with amusement at my new look than their own relief at not being singled out.

"No, ma'am."

"Very good, then," she said, still staring at my hair as if trying to determine what I'd been going for. "Fifteen hundred words, everyone." She put her hand on my shoulder as she turned to cast her gaze over the thirty students quietly mouthing curse words into their spiral notebooks. "And try to write something that won't make me want to stab myself in the eye."

• • •

The reactions of subsequent students and teachers to my new celebrity look (including singsong calls of "Loooocy!" in the hallways) were, if anything, even less auspicious. But this public humiliation was, I reassured myself, simply a test. Stars were trendsetters, and clearly, I was surrounded by people afraid to reinvent themselves. Those who bucked conventionality were often derided—until the moment when their star ascended and the naysayers found themselves groveling at the foot of the indifferent luminary. Although I constantly debated the merits of returning to my former cow-patty color, doing so would be a dramatic admission of failure, a clear signal of disbelief in the Manilow magic I was attempting to project. I would have to tough it out.

The next ten days raced by in a blur as I worked to further prepare, both internally and externally, for my potential moment in the sun. In a bid to replicate a pop star wardrobe, I made a pilgrimage to St. Louis's most sophisticated men's store, Chess King. There, with money from Mother and Dad (who understood the importance of investing in talent), I purchased a pair of tight black bell-bottoms and a red polyester shirt that glowed like satin.

"What do you think?" I said to Val as I waltzed into her bedroom, proudly modeling the outfit.

"What are you," she said, glancing up from her *Cosmo* quiz, "a flamenco dancer?"

Deflated, I turned to leave.

"Oh, I'm kidding," she said, softening. "It's nice. But maybe you could exchange the shirt for another color? That one just emphasizes the fright wig on your head."

All of this preparation had taken a huge bite out of my available book report time, and before I knew it, it was Thursday. *The Grapes of Wrath* was due tomorrow—and I had not even cracked the book.

I began to panic as the implications hit me full in the face.

I had never failed an assignment. What would this do to my *smell me* 3.8 grade point average? What would this do to the compliments about me that I imagined were bandied about by Mrs. Campbell in the teacher's lounge? "That Eric Poole is quite the gifted one, isn't he? His essays give me *such* a thrill."

And then it came to me. The bookstore at Cross Keys shopping center had a selection of Cliff's Notes, those handy booklets that precluded the need to actually read a novel. Could *The Grapes of Wrath* be among them?

I borrowed Dad's car and raced up to Cross Keys, skulking into the bookstore, my head whirling around like a police car light as I scanned the aisles for potential spies. And there it was, on a black metal rack, its neon-yellow cover calling out to me with its siren song.

I really had no choice, I reasoned, but to take a shortcut.

• • •

The *Grapes of Wrath* essay I ended up producing was an astute, insightful treatise on the themes of man's inhumanity to man and the saving power of family and fellowship. Although the use of this "study guide" was, perhaps, morally ambiguous, I couldn't risk disappointing Mrs. Campbell, who, I imagined, sat down with my English papers like other women did a box of Godiva chocolates.

And more importantly, I couldn't risk disappointing my Stage Band comrades, who I was certain were counting on me to deliver the goods. But thanks to this time-saving tome, which had allowed me many extra hours of trumpet practice, my solo at the Stage Band competition would indeed be Barry-worthy.

Years from now, I thought, my fans and I will chortle at the outrageous stunts I'd had to pull in the pursuit of my creative vision, and I imagined retelling this story in the Oscar-winning rockumentary that would be made about my ascent to stardom. Clearly, the end justified the means, since as a pop superstar, I would be able to impact the lives—and morals—of millions of fans, encouraging *them* to be ethical and principled in their pursuit of greatness.

The bell rang, indicating the end of first period.

"Eric, could you stay after class?"

Mrs. Campbell smiled at me. *She must want to congratulate me on a paper well done,* I thought. But as much as I lived for these moments of praise, I really didn't want her to make a big deal out of this particular book report.

"Oh, thanks," I said, returning the smile, "but my second period is all the way across the building. I should—"

"Sit," she ordered.

Mrs. C waited patiently for the other students to bustle out. I watched her craggy face, which suddenly seemed to reflect less a sense of pride and scholarly kinship than one of annoyance. As the last student exited, she closed the door. And locked it.

"Uh," I said, a bit nervous now, "aren't your second-period students gonna need to get in?"

"They'll wait," she said dismissively as she clomped across the room in her heavy Pilgrim pumps and took a backward seat at the desk in front of me. The expression beneath her blondish-brown bangs was ominous.

"So, tell me," she said as she handed me my book report. "What on earth made you think you'd get away with this?"

A large, red F was scrawled across the top of the page. I blanched. Apparently, there would be no high-fiving, no secret confessions of favoritism, no suggestions that someone of my intellectual caliber be graduated early. This would not be in the rockumentary.

"What—what do you mean?" I said nervously.

"You know, if you were gonna cheat," she said evenly, "the least you could have done was not do it so blatantly."

Sweat began to trickle down my forehead.

"You lifted entire chunks from the *Grapes of Wrath* Cliff's Notes—verbatim. Couldn't you have at least taken the time to rewrite a sentence here and there? My *god*." She shook her head. "You know, this isn't exactly my first time at the rodeo."

I didn't know what calf roping had to do with English papers, but in the moment, I let it go. I sat there, ashamed at both my malfeasance and my stupidity at getting caught. I had never cheated before. But this act of duplicity had, after all, been a necessary evil in my pursuit of a Manilow-size life.

"Aside from what this will do to your grade," she barked, "I'm gonna have to report you to the principal. You'll be suspended."

"No!" I said before I could stop myself. "I have to play at the state Stage Band competition next week. It's my chance to—"

I stopped.

"Your chance to what?"

I respected Mrs. C, I wanted to please her, but I didn't really feel close to her. And I certainly couldn't admit how much I had pinned my hopes on my moment in the Stage Band sun.

"I'm… I'm good at the trumpet," I said hesitantly.

"I know," she replied. "I chaperoned the dance where you played your first solo last year. Your chance to what?" she said.

"Nothing," I said. "I'm sorry about the book report. I'll do it over. Or I'll do a different book. Whatever you want. Just please don't turn me in!"

"Your chance to what?" she said, her apparently-broken-in-a-bar-fight nose twitching with irritation. "Answer the question."

I paused and looked away. Admitting this felt harder than admitting to cheating. "To be somebody, I guess," I mumbled.

"And you think you're gonna become somebody by taking shortcuts? Is that how you think life works?"

I stared silently down at the beige laminate desktop. "I'm sorry about the Cliff's Notes," I said quietly.

There was a long, uncomfortable pause as she gazed at me. Finally, she spoke.

"I know you are." Her voice softened ever so slightly. "Tell you what. I won't report you to Principal Nibley. You'll still get an F on this paper. But you'll be able to go to the Stage Band competition."

I smiled at her gratefully, tears starting to form in my eyes. "Thank you. I'm really sorry. I wouldn't have done it, but I—"

She held up her hand to silence me. "Don't insult me by making excuses." Her stern look returned. "You'll also do another book report, due in two weeks, on *Of Mice and Men*."

"Yes, ma'am."

"I'm also gonna recommend that you be disqualified for the *I Dare You* Award. I'm sure you'd agree that this is not the kind of thing that should be rewarded."

"Well," I said, trying to lighten the moment, "it *was* daring."

She rose, stone-faced. "Eric, you were nominated because we want to reward kids who strive to be their best and inspire others. And I see some real leadership potential in you. Deep down. But this," she said, pointing to my paper, "is not the behavior of a leader. You're dismissed."

I gathered my books and hurried to the door.

"By the way," she called after me, pointing to my head, "I know you kids are all about self-expression, but Jesus."

• • •

A few days later, the twenty-some members of the Stage Band piled onto the grimy school bus excitedly, grateful for the opportunity to create nerd mayhem in another city, the possibility of a trophy looming large in our minds. There was a lot of whooping and hollering, trombone and flute players alike buzzing with the happy knowledge that on this bus ride, unlike the daily ones to and from school, no one would be made to cry.

I, on the other hand, was still stinging from my fall from grace. Yet I knew that I had to set my regret aside and focus on the moment that could make me a star. Barry Manilow had suffered setbacks in his rise to fame—he started as Bette Midler's pianist and now they were no longer speaking. This was, I told myself, simply one of mine.

At least I had Mitch there to support me.

"I'm glad we get to do this together," I said as he sat down in the seat I'd saved for him for in the middle of the bus. (The high-status back rows were, of course, reserved for drummers.)

"This is gonna be such a big day."

"I know," he replied. "Just think—if we win, it'll be something to tell our kids." He glanced at me. "Are you okay? You seem nervous or something."

"I guess I am, a little," I replied, as I unconsciously rehearsed my trumpet fingerings. "I mean, it's my moment."

"Your moment to what?"

"Well, you know, to become a star."

"Huh?"

"My solo. This could put me over the top."

"The top of what?"

I sighed heavily at Mitch's obtuseness. But I really couldn't blame him. As someone rather marginally talented, he couldn't possibly understand the opportunities that lay before someone like me.

"Don't be scared," he reassured me. "Pete has a solo, too. And John. They're not nervous."

Mr. Ronson stood up from his seat behind the bus driver and quieted us. He was a large, burly man with a graying crew cut and a love for music—even when it was being played by boobs marching the wrong way on the football field.

"I just want to tell you kids," he said, smiling, "how proud I am of you."

We all beamed. Mr. Ronson's occasional *Hindenburg* moments aside, he was a beloved leader.

"We're gonna go in there and carpet-bomb those idiots like we used to do the Vietcong," he bellowed over the belching roar of the bus engine. A cheer went up.

"And even if we get creamed," he added as the cheer sputtered out, "we can walk away with our heads held high. Well, not as high as if we place. But, you know, high enough."

The day was cool and cloudy as we arrived at Kirksville High. I vowed to take in every detail of the day: the hordes of nervous, excited teens pouring off buses, the San Quentin–inspired concrete block hallways, and the gymnasium fragrant with the odor of sweat socks and unwashed jocks—a smell that typically threw me into a panic, but one that, today, seemed like the wondrously heady fumes of a trophy that has been freshly painted gold.

Each band took its seats in the bleachers, huddling together to assess and trash talk the competition, careful to applaud the absolute minimum that civility required. The air in the gym was cold and clammy, but nerves had taken hold of me and I was sweating like a pig on luau day.

Our Stage Band was fourth, smack in the middle of the competition. Bands number one through three were fairly solid, with an occasional standout member soloing on the sax or drums on songs like "Boogie Fever" and "Turn the Beat Around." The audience clapped loudly for these artists, feeling less inhibited about celebrating individual musicians who didn't play their instrument.

"Man, this sucks," I whispered to Mitch as he absentmindedly licked his reed.

"What does?"

"Pete and John are totally outclassed. God, I hope this doesn't blow our chances. I really need this win."

"For what?"

"For my *career*. This could launch me."

"Jeez," Mitch replied, a little taken aback, "I didn't realize that we were all here just to support you."

"That's not what I mean," I said defensively, as various band members shushed us. "But, you know, there *are* certain key members of the band…"

"And what, you're number one on that list?"

"Well…" I said modestly.

"What is going on with you?" he snapped. "I hate to tell you this, but it's news to me, and probably everybody else, that this is your 'star turn.' You are not *that special*."

"Next up," the emcee announced, "is Hazelwood Central High School from Fluorescent, Missouri!"

"It's Florissant!" Mr. Ronson screamed. "*Flor*-is-sent!"

As we rose and clomped across the bleachers and onto the gymnasium floor, I felt as if I was having an out-of-body experience. Was Mitch just jealous? I wondered. Was he trying to sabotage me? I wondered if these were the words Bette Midler had spat at my doppelgänger. How had he reacted?

"Dear God," I said in silent prayer as we took our places, "please help me to overlook the spitefulness of my friend. Help me to rise above his pettiness and become the star I am meant to be."

Mr. Ronson mimed a bomb blast and raised his baton. *Don't let negativity distract you*, I told myself.

We launched into our first song, the disco version of the *Star Wars* theme. The nonrhythm and woodwind members of the audience roared their calculatedly restrained approval at John's drum and Pete's sax solos.

We finished to a level of applause that was, I calculated, 10 to 15 percent higher than most other bands. I glanced up at the bleachers. Kids stared icily down at us, a gratifying sign.

My solo was in our second number, the one I felt would secure our place in the annals of Stage Band competitions— the superpopular *Rocky* theme, "Gonna Fly Now." It was a big number—confident, bold, larger-than-life.

And I am, I thought as we began to play the majestic

opening to the song, *in my element. This is the place I feel at home. This is the place I know how to shine. I* am *special here.* I would show Mitch.

As I counted down to my solo, I took a deep breath. This moment would require improvisational runs that reached into the stratosphere of high notes, that dog-pitch arena where trumpeters really shined. That, I knew, was trophy land.

I began with a two-octave-spanning sequence that provoked an impressive smattering of applause, which buoyed me.

And as two bars became four, I began to relax a bit. I was playing well—perhaps even beautifully. I could feel the energy of the band backing me, willing me to go higher. And I would do my best to oblige them. I closed my eyes and envisioned spinning newspapers, their headlines touting the birth of a star.

As four impressive bars became eight, I launched into the finale of my solo, blasting for the treetops with a series of high notes.

Although I had always been good at improvisation, high Cs were my weak spot. But this day, this moment, I seemed to be lifted by angels. I almost effortlessly managed a high B. Emboldened, I shot for the C, one step up. It pierced the clammy air like a brilliant foghorn. I was in historic territory, here. I would go for one more.

In my final passage, I executed a high D. And hit it.

The audience roared its approval. This was not the polite applause other soloists had enjoyed. This was the appreciation of musicians who realized they were in the presence of greatness.

I beamed a gracious smile to indicate my humility and turned to smirk at Mitch.

He rolled his eyes.

• • •

Mitch and I sat on opposite ends of the bleachers as our group gauged the competition of the next five bands. Although still stinging from his callousness, I was on a Manilow high. And I was determined to rub his face in it.

I loudly accepted the elbowed congratulations of my bandmates with a delicious sense of both fulfillment and righteousness, as Mitch fiddled with his clarinet and pretended not to notice.

The crowd was now thinning considerably as members of the audience convened outside to smoke and bad-mouth other groups. But I remained in the bleachers in order to soak up the hateful looks of competing trumpet players.

The final band of the day assembled on the floor, a largely black-populated band. They were an inner-city group whose facilities and educators were, I assumed, lacking in quality, and this would likely reflect in their performance. I felt for them. They, like me, were probably always being dismissed and disregarded. I resolved to cheer them on.

As they launched into their first song, the Sylvers' "Boogie Fever," I was, I had to admit, a bit startled by their sound. They seemed to be extremely well rehearsed. Score one, I thought, for the underdogs.

This song relied heavily on brass instrumentation, and their trumpet and trombone players were impressive. Tight and seemingly effortless, they even danced—with Temptations-style moves that, although dated for my taste, were executed with drill-team precision.

Members of our group began glancing at one another. Less than a minute into their first song, it was already becoming clear: this was a band to be reckoned with.

They finished "Boogie Fever" to some of the weakest applause of the day, the audience determined not to sway the judges' opinions by giving them the kudos they deserved. This was a band, I thought with both admiration and irritation, that could easily be playing weddings at a Holiday Inn. Maybe even a Sheraton.

As they launched into their second song, the Stevie Wonder hit "Sir Duke," the judges bobbed their heads in time to the song, and I began to realize that our win—or at least a high-placing finish—was now in jeopardy. Hoping to spark a mass audience exodus, I rose to exit.

Mr. Ronson, seated behind me, grabbed my belt loop and yanked me down. "Does that sound like it's over?"

I sighed and begrudgingly lowered myself onto the bench, just as an elfin trumpet player raised his horn to his lips.

I had weathered any number of trumpet solos that day, coming out what I felt was the clear winner. This was my moment, and it seemed only a matter of time before I would launch a stunning solo career. I wondered if I would have to forgo college, since my public would likely demand it.

I had not, however, weathered a solo like this. That unassuming kid—a combination of Maynard Ferguson and Miles Davis—was, like me, an improviser. And an extraordinary one. As he began to play, blazing across octaves with scatting runs of amazing complexity, I was aghast. And confused.

What was happening?

Within four bars it was apparent that he was light-years ahead of most of the trumpet players in the room. And as his solo continued—with moments of sublime melody followed by punchy percussive blasts that seemed utterly effortless—it became apparent that he was also light-years ahead of me.

And at one point, as he took a pause to breathe, the bleachers burst into applause. Panicked, I glanced around to assess the audience. People were sitting up straight, leaning forward so as not to miss a note.

The world seemed to be imploding around me. I could barely process what was transpiring. His solo seemed to go on forever, obviously goaded on by a notoriety-obsessed band director who knew that this kid was his ace in the hole.

When he finally finished—on a high E, besting not only my solo but my top note—the audience fairly exploded in a rafter-shaking cheer and leaped to their feet.

• • •

I sat alone in the bus seat, staring out the window at the cows and wheat fields rushing past. I was reminded of my childhood, when Dad would point to cows and say, "That's a pig," mislabeling all manner of livestock until my first-grade teacher called my parents in, concerned that I was adding a learning disability to my illustrious list of inadequacies.

The merriment of the morning had given way to a sullen silence. We had not won. We had not even placed second or third. But the band's loss meant little to me in this moment. I had suffered a greater one—a loss of identity. I had been outplayed by a kid who was, to add insult to injury, a year younger than me.

It had truly never occurred to me that there would be someone out there more talented than me. And if there was someone more talented within the state of *Missouri*, I thought, imagine how many there might be in the other forty-nine states. Although some of the southern ones probably didn't count.

It seemed dizzyingly, crushingly clear: I was no Barry Manilow. And never would be. I felt abandoned—by both my dreams and the God who had given them to me.

"Move over."

Mitch was standing in the aisle of the creaking school bus. I grudgingly moved a few inches over, and he sat down next to me, but I refused to look at him. He had obviously come to gloat. And I guess I couldn't blame him.

I stared out the window, too defeated to even be angry, as we sat in silence for a long moment.

"I didn't stand, you know."

"What?" I said, trying to sound as annoyed as possible.

"When that guy played his solo. I didn't stand."

If anything, this made me feel worse. Because more than ever, I realized that I had acted like a pompous jerk. In this moment, I wanted to thank Mitch for being my friend, for still liking me even if I wasn't better than him. I wanted to let him know how much that small act of kindness meant to me.

But I was ashamed.

• • •

"And finally," Principal Nibley declared, wrapping up his morning announcements with a madcap tone of despair, "we have a winner for the William Danforth *I Dare You* Award. Doris?"

His assistant, Doris, switched on a cassette tape recorder that played a tinny drum roll as he announced, in a voice that could have been reciting a list of the dead after a nuclear accident, "Eric Poole."

There was a small gasp in Mrs. Campbell's English class as my tangerine-tinged head—currently hovering just above the surface of my desk—jerked upright.

"Wow, congratulations!" Shelly whispered.

This has to be a mistake, I thought, searching Mrs. C's face for an answer. I had been humiliatingly disqualified. Over a band competition that I had, in no uncertain terms, lost.

"Mr. Nibley would like to see you in his office," Mrs. Campbell said, with no discernable tone of either joy or judgment.

Still in shock, I grabbed my books and hustled to the door. As I crossed into the hall, Mrs. C followed me and closed the door behind her.

"You didn't disqualify me?" I whispered, bewildered.

She shook her head and glanced around to see who else was in the hallway. It was deserted. "Mr. Ronson told me what happened at the band competition."

I looked down, embarrassed. There was an awkward moment of silence.

"I guess," she said gently, "I just wanted you to know that you *are* somebody."

Then, as if embarrassed by her own kindness, she turned abruptly on her heel. "Even with that hair."

I unconsciously touched my head as she clomped back into the classroom, the door slowly closing behind her.

As I headed downstairs to the principal's office, my faith

began to blossom anew. Maybe I still had *some* sort of star potential. Even if I couldn't see it, maybe God could.

Maybe he was trying to tell me that it just wasn't meant to be in music. I was creative—I would come up with a new outlet for my gifts. I would find someone new to be.

As I descended to the first floor, I began to envision the opportunities that might come with this prestigious national recognition. Much like Miss America, I might have to tour the country, opening supermarkets and ghetto housing projects. I wondered if there was a monetary prize—I was gonna need a lot more Sun-In. Would my picture be on the front page of the *Post-Dispatch* this weekend, I wondered? I would need to buy a dozen copies to send to relatives and people I hated.

As I entered the office, I smiled proudly at Doris, the cranky secretary who always seemed to be under the impression that she was guarding the president.

"What are you doing here? Class is in session," she snapped. "State your business."

"I'm Eric Poole," I said tentatively. "Mrs. Campbell told me to—"

"Oh, right," she replied, pointing to Mr. Nibley's office door. "You may enter."

I crossed to his office and took a deep breath, opening the door slowly since, I calculated, it might be crowded with dignitaries.

Mr. Nibley was sitting at his desk, alone, eating a strawberry Pop-Tart.

"Yes?"

"I'm Eric Poole."

"Oh. Right. Hang on." He wiped the frosting off his hands and handed me a small book entitled *I Dare You*, by William Danforth, and a sturdy piece of paper on which was stamped my name and some sort of official seal.

"Here you go. Congratulations."

I looked at him blankly. "Is, um, Mr. Danforth here?"

"Who?" He took another bite. "Oh, he's dead."

"Well, thank you," I replied, unsure what to do. "Is there a ceremony I need to attend at the capitol, or…?"

"Nah. Every school gives one of these out."

"Oh. So…"

"So, enjoy." He took another bite of his Pop-Tart. "Go out there and dare people. Or something."

Chapter 3

THESE BOOTS WERE MADE FOR STEALIN'

"Shh!" I yelled as the pair of shoe boxes Teddy was pushing into the loading dock hallway toppled over, and knee-high boots and Earth shoes tumbled across the concrete floor. "Dale's gonna hear!"

Teddy recklessly gathered our bounty and threw the shoes into their boxes as I frantically listened for the sound of a toilet flushing, wondering exactly how I had gotten myself into this mess.

It had all begun some months before, as I had cast about in search of someone new to be. Despondent over my Stage Band loss and disillusioned with a high school world that seemed to be celebrating my anonymity, I had no idea what my place was or how to elevate myself beyond the miserable station at which I resided.

But one day, as I crept through the halls of Hazelwood

Central attempting to avoid a Tony Tropler skirmish, I began to notice that the majority of my classmates possessed a distinct lack of personal style. I was sporting a supertrendy Calvin Klein earth-tone banded-collar shirt and off-white Jeans West onionskin jacket, and I positively reeked of the sophisticated cologne by designer Pierre Cardin. Most of them were wearing Target. And Brut.

Perhaps, I began to consider, as a man of inordinately good taste, the persona I was truly meant to embody was that of someone like Halston, the red-hot fashion designer who had virtually become American royalty. Halston was a Midwestern lad like me who had been vaulted into the stratosphere by power brokers who recognized his trendsetting talents.

Expressing the characteristics of Halston, I thought, would provide me the kind of distinctive persona certain to set me apart from the madding crowd. Sure, there were other smart kids at school, other talented musicians, but did they also possess a keen fashion sense?

From what I could gather from magazine photos, Halston's aesthetic seemed to be all about simplicity and cigarettes, so I cast aside the accessories so currently in vogue among my band friends, opting for a classier, more streamlined look (no puka-shell necklace would detract from *my* polyester disco shirt), along with—when Mother, Dad, and Val weren't around—an oft-present cigarette. These urbane elements were sure to result in my being whisked off to New York City to party at Studio 54 with Liza Minnelli, a scenario that appealed to me on more levels than I even cared to consider.

Seeing Halston holding a cigarette in virtually every magazine photo gave this disgusting habit a heretofore unrecognized sheen of glamour. But since I despised the smell of smoke, and since I couldn't risk Mother and Dad smelling it on my clothes, I elected to merely hold a cigarette in my hand and declare that I was "trying to quit." I chose Kool 100s as my brand, since their menthol smelled like a Halls cough drop, and since they had thoughtfully spelled out their sophistication right in the name.

I also began auditioning buzzwords to sprinkle into my everyday speech—"That coat is fabulous!" "I am simply agog!"—until one of the guys in my theater class commented that I needed to reel it in a little.

Mother and Dad seemed patently unaware of the hipster in their midst.

"What difference does it make what shoes you're wearing?" Dad said as I stood in front of the full-length mirror inside the coat closet, wearing a pair of oversized sunglasses and modeling my third pair of platform shoes. "Those bell-bottoms cover the whole shoe."

"You might as well be wearing Val's fuzzy slippers," Mother added. "Who would know?"

"What about when I sit down?" I snapped. "Would you like me to be *humiliated*? Clearly," I announced as I clomped back down the hall toward my bedroom, "there's only one person with panache in this house."

The problem was that expressing all this classiness required cash. Those Chess King faux-suede leisure suits and fifty-cent packs of cigs weren't just gonna buy themselves. In order to fully articulate my sixteen-year-old creativity and selflessly serve as a model for the flair impaired, I was going to need a part-time job.

Of course, the thought of laboring in some sweatshop held little appeal. As a fashion icon whose artistic vision could only be nurtured by thousands of hours of lying in front of the TV, I was understandably reticent to undermine my opportunities for inspiration by spending my weekends working a fry vat.

But money was not exactly flowing into my coffers. Although I still performed chores for which I was duly paid by Mother and Dad, this was pocket change compared to the tens of dollars I now required. After all, friends frequently commented on my daring mix of design elements—"I would never in a million years have put that outfit together," "You really like to take chances, don't you?" "I didn't realize they made those for men"—and having real money could catapult my reputation as a suburban style setter to the next level.

Becoming a member of the workforce would, I realized, have one additional benefit: it would get me out of the house and away from the primal-scream therapy sessions Mother conducted promptly at 6:30 p.m. each night, when she returned home from work.

"God in heaven!" she would shriek, raising her fists to the sky as Val and I scattered to our bedrooms. It had always been unclear to me whether the airborne fisticuffs were merely meant to punctuate her words or if she was actually threatening to punch out the Lord Jesus. *Why are there crumbs on this counter?!!*

Dad, a thoughtless swine who seemed patently unable to prepare dinner while simultaneously keeping the kitchen pristine enough to serve as a hospital operating room, would sigh.

"Elaine…"

"I ask so little!" she would cry, dissolving into tears, a martyr for the cause of home sanitation.

In my childhood years, this was typically the point where my heart would soften. *She's just trying to keep a nice home*, I would think, refusing to allow the experience of hundreds of previous nights to color my reasoning.

"If the soap dish in that bathroom has scum in it," she would bellow at Val and me, slamming down her purse and shifting back into overdrive, "you'd better sleep with one eye open!"

And thus it was decided: I would join the working world.

I began a search for the perfect position, one that would alternately showcase my burgeoning élan and require little if any actual labor. Given my deep understanding of the importance of footwear, I finally settled on a position at Thom McAn, a popular chain store that featured high-heeled tennis shoes and waffle stomper boots. This was an environment, I decided, in which I, as the Halston of Hazelwood Central, could flower, a bastion of high style where work would feel like anything but, as I counseled ladies of leisure on their fashion footwear needs.

● ● ●

"It's your turn to clean the toilet."

Dale, the Thom McAn manager, a dark-haired, wiry guy with a black mustache and modified mutton chops, sauntered into the stockroom where I was unpacking a shipment of boxes.

Although this bathroom hygiene duty—as well as the stockroom work—had been mentioned fleetingly in the interview, I had airily assumed that my demand as a fashion guru would trump any requests of this nature and result in a lifetime ban on my having to kneel over a filthy commode or wield a box cutter.

To my dismay, after three weeks, I hadn't even made it out to the sales floor.

"The best way for you to learn the shoe business," Dale had explained with the sagacity of someone who had risen to the lofty heights of shoe store management, "is from the sole up."

Now, as I knelt on the floor, unpacking a giant crate of penny loafers and sweating in my fashion-forward Merry-Go-Round corduroy blazer, Dale leaned against one of the rolling ladders that were attached to the twelve-foot-high shelving units.

"I don't know what Teddy had for lunch, but *Jesus*." He tossed me a pine-scented car air freshener on a string. "Hang this around your neck before you go in there."

I wiped the perspiration from my brow as Dale smiled magnanimously. "You can take your jacket off this time." He handed me the toilet brush. "Don't want you to get crap on the corduroy."

"This isn't the kind of thing I would have to do," I said, trying to camouflage my hauteur, "if I worked in the City."

"There aren't any Thom McAns in the city," Dale replied.

"I mean The City. New York…?"

"You used to live in New York?"

"No, I just—never mind."

Thus far, the only saving grace of the job had been Teddy, a quick-witted seventeen-year-old from school. Teddy played drums in marching band and had obviously selected this instrument for its ability to attract girls, since drummers were considered the superstuds of band. This helped only marginally, however, since he sported an impressive Jewfro (although he wasn't Jewish), and his mismatched wardrobe gave him the appearance of a special-needs student.

"We gotta get better jobs," he would mutter as we unloaded a pallet of women's clear-heeled sling backs while Dale sat "doing the schedule," which took hours, given that he spent most of it reading *Letters to Penthouse*. "Maybe cleaning up crime scenes. Probably doesn't pay that great," he whispered as he nodded in Dale's direction, "but all the people you want to kill are already dead."

"Nah, we gotta hang in there," I replied with certainty. "Once we get out on the floor, it'll all be worth it."

The floor was where I would realize my potential. Where customers would clamor for my fashion advice. Where Bianca Jagger or Jackie O would sweep in to buy some glitter wedges and end up begging to take me to Corsica on their yachts.

It was also where the money was. My three-dollar-an-hour base wage really didn't add up to much—it was the commission that would send my salary into the stratosphere of minimum-wage workers, the element that would make this job exponentially more profitable than Pledging the paneling at home. Working an average of eighteen hours a week, I estimated that I'd eventually be earning upward of sixty dollars after taxes.

Unfortunately, as I was about to discover, it wasn't enough.

• • •

"Your mother lost her job today."

Val and I stood in the family room staring at our father, stunned.

"How could that be?" I replied. "Aren't they *scared* of her?"

The ubiquitous Reverend B. R. Tibbits, whose reel-to-reel sermons blasted through the house day and night, declared that wives were the property of their husbands, but in our family, it was more than clear who was in charge. And I presumed the same went for Mother's employer.

"Life," Dad explained, ignoring my editorializing, "is a spiritual battle, a war in which we, as Christian soldiers, must do battle with the forces of evil that conspire against us."

"So Mother's boss is the enemy?" I asked.

"Well, no."

"The company is a minion of Satan?"

"Not exactly."

"Well, then, who's she at war with?"

Dad looked stumped. "It'll all be explained when we get to heaven." He collapsed into his La-Z-Boy.

I wondered what Mother's arrival that evening would bring. Would there be the usual cries to the heavens when she realized no one had vacuumed the garage? Or would this be the event that finally pushed her over the edge? I considered duct-taping leftover orange basement carpet tiles to my torso to serve as a flak jacket should she attempt to mow down the family in a hail of gunfire.

Mother had always been difficult—her hair-trigger temper at home and her periodic condescension to unsuspecting members of the public were legendary. As children, she had instilled in us—via a highly effective campaign of terror—a commitment to cleansing that would have impressed Hitler.

"If there are footprints in that living room shag," she'd intone at a level of hysteria usually reserved for the outbreak of plagues in the Middle Ages, "you'd better start boning up on the foster care system."

But she had, nonetheless, always been there for Val and me. We knew that in her mind we were indolent slugs who lacked her astounding work ethic, but we also knew that she loved us madly in spite of these prodigious shortcomings. And now that we were young adults, her periodic tantrums were less frightening than simply exasperating. She no longer terrified us so much as annoyed the hell out of us.

Thus, her entrance an hour later—which bore all the markings of a state funeral—was shocking. There was no screaming, no crying, simply a leaden stillness. And suddenly, the strong, independent woman I had seen for sixteen years began to crumble.

"Would you like some brussels sprout casserole?" I said brightly, passing the Corningware dish to Mother as we all sat at the dinner table.

She smiled wanly and shook her head, nibbling half-heartedly at a leaf of lettuce, a meal less than half the size of her normal ones. I stared down at my plate, swirling my casserole haphazardly with my fork, unable to bear her expression. Rather than revel in her experience of what it was like to be on the other side of the failure equation, I wanted nothing more than to hug her.

But we didn't do that.

• • •

Teddy and I graduated to the Thom McAn sales floor. This only partially diminished our backroom duties, but any relief was welcome. Teddy was a natural salesman, joking with customers, egging them on to purchase second pairs and expensive accessories.

Being pushy did not, however, come naturally to me. This initially gave me pause, but I quickly reassured myself that unerring taste was a far greater talent than sales ability. Would Halston be caught dead hawking heel savers?

"You're just too nice," Dale said as we stood smoking in the stockroom.

"My focus," I explained as I exhaled deeply from my unlit Kool, "is helping people make the correct fashion choice."

"Fashion, smashion," Dale replied, blowing actual smoke out of his nose. "You gotta be more aggressive. Think of this place like a slaughterhouse. The customers are stupid, some of 'em stink, and they don't know what's coming. Then all of a sudden, BAM!"

But no matter how hard I tried, selling was a chore. My dream of customers gratefully soaking up my fashion wisdom was quickly becoming a nightmare of middle-aged women—who at some point in their lives or imaginations had possessed the measurements of Malibu Barbie and were hell-bent on maintaining the illusion—demanding that I wedge their now-sausage-like appendages into pumps three sizes too small. Requesting a shoe larger than a seven appeared to be an admission of defeat akin to the surrender of troops at Appomattox.

Dale, whose vast treasure trove of insight into women was on regular display when we were standing in the back room out of their earshot, explained, "All chicks want big tits and tiny toes." He took a drag off his Parliament. "It's in their DNA."

The male customers weren't much better. I found myself spending the majority of my time arguing with old men who attempted to return shoes apparently worn to Eisenhower's inauguration.

And to top things off, my sales ineptitude had resulted in commission checks that typically added only pennies to my hourly wage. Dale, whether through blind determination or tragically misguided optimism, refused to accept that he could not turn me into a model salesman.

"In six or eight years, if you work really hard," he would tell me as we closed up the store after a grueling day of smelling feet and accepting limp cash pulled from sweaty cleavage, "I could see you *assistant managing* this store."

This did little to assuage my growing realization that shoe selling was neither the most fulfilling or profitable means of expressing one's inner Halston-ness. After shelling out for car insurance, meals, and a small but stylistically significant selection of clip-on ties, it felt like I barely had enough left over for Kools.

● ● ●

Mother soldiered on after her job loss, immediately signing up with a temp agency. Her current position was at an ad agency downtown, which was a long drive from North St. Louis County, so to save money, she took the bus, which required a nearly ninety-minute journey each direction.

This made her workdays twelve hours long, and when she arrived home each night she was utterly drained. At first, I assumed that the delightful cessation of her nightly performances of *The Sound and the Fury* was due to exhaustion, but a query about her employment clarified the reason.

"How's the job?" I asked one night, hoping to hear that they had hired her full-time and promoted her to CEO.

"I hate it," she replied, startling me with such a frank reply. "It's such tedious work—filing, taking dictation. I thought I was beyond this." She paused and added softly, almost to herself, "And they're so unfriendly. *Nobody* talks to me."

The fact that she was being forced into menial work that she hadn't had to perform in years was sad enough, but knowing that she felt ostracized broke my heart. My childhood had been a buffet of banishment and isolation. I knew a little something about that.

• • •

"You ever feel like we're indentured servants?" I said to Teddy one December afternoon as we restocked the women's boots while the Salsoul Orchestra's Christmas album played over the store sound system.

"Yeah," he mumbled. "I thought I was gonna be able to buy a car with this job. But I can't even afford a Chevette, much less a Firebird like yours."

I may have neglected to mention to Teddy that the car I drove was not actually mine, an oversight that had prompted more than one hysterical moment when Mother suggested I drive Dad's Pontiac Catalina to work instead.

The lid on a shoe box fell off. I paused for a moment, staring at the expensive knee-high boots inside, supple leather atop pristine heels. I knew that these were the kind of boots Mother should be seen in. But she certainly couldn't afford them right now, and neither could I.

"Boy, I wish…" I said softly, unaware that I was even speaking the words aloud.

Teddy smirked. "We don't have your size."

I pulled one out of the box and held it up. "My mother would die." I sighed.

I envisioned her waltzing into the ad agency in her new high-style boots, the bosses whistling and whispering to one another, "This chick is somebody to be reckoned with."

"Welcome to the club, Elaine," I imagined one of the women in the typing pool announcing as she and the other girls presented her with a plaque. "We're so sorry we were such bitches."

"Whoever chose those boots," the CEO would say, "is a man of real taste."

"I know," Teddy replied, jolting me back into reality. "I want to get my dad a pair of Earth shoes, but it's either that or lunches." Teddy stood up. "Let's take a break."

We grabbed our coats and walked out the back door and down the hallway to the empty loading dock. I placed a flattened boot box lid on the cement, topped it with a paper towel, and carefully lowered myself onto it. Teddy rolled his eyes and plopped down on the pavement next to me as we dangled our legs over the dock.

"Exactly when," he asked, as I removed a Kool from the jacket pocket of my three-piece suit and held it haughtily between my index and middle fingers, "did you *start* smoking?"

"Don't be gauche." I inhaled from the unlit cigarette and glanced around. I had never really noticed before how quiet it was. Few cars passed by. No other workers from the neighboring shops seemed to hang out back here.

"Boy," I said, jokingly as I exhaled, "I'm surprised people don't steal stuff from these stores. Nobody'd ever see it back here."

There was a long, uncomfortable pause. Teddy glanced around. "Especially at night."

Our eyes locked and, in a rush of telepathic communication, we transmitted our mutually illicit thoughts.

"We couldn't," he said.

"It's wrong," I said.

"'Course, as hard as we work…"

"And as little as they pay us…"

"It's really like getting the raise we should have gotten months ago."

"Yeah," I said. "They owe us."

Within minutes, we had mapped out a plan.

• • •

Dale, Teddy, and I were closing the store. Tonight was the night, and I was not at all sure that I wanted to go through with this.

Teddy winked at me. If he had serious reservations, he was hiding them well. "We're stickin' it to The Man," he had said repeatedly over the past couple of weeks, apparently seeing us as some sort of Symbionese Liberation Army for shoes.

A few minutes earlier, when the store was empty and Dale was in the bathroom peeing, Teddy had furtively hidden our bounty outside the back door, in the hallway that led to the loading dock, as I stood guard. As he pushed them into the hallway, the boxes had tumbled over, and Teddy had had to recover their contents in the frantic moments before Dale emerged from the john.

If Dale caught us, we'd be fired and would likely end up in prison trying to make a shiv out of a Gee Your Hair Smells Terrific shampoo bottle. But this mission was critical; I was, after all, a tastemaker whose fashion choices would be greeted with hosannas by my mother when she realized that I had not only brightened an otherwise bleak Christmas but also heightened her fashion street cred. *And this isn't really theft*, I reassured myself. *It's more like I'm Halston Hood—stealing from the rich to aid the unfashionably attired.*

Fortunately, Dale had been too busy missing the toilet bowl and combing his mustache to get wise to the criminal proceedings taking place fifty feet away. Now, as we flipped off the lights and Dale locked the door, Teddy yawned theatrically.

"Whoo!" he hollered. "I'm bushed. We worked like *dogs* today."

"Yeah," I added. "We really earned our pay. And *then* some."

Dale rolled his eyes and lit up a Parliament. "Uh-huh. You were a regular chain gang."

The three of us began walking together to the parking lot, Teddy and I purposely lagging behind Dale.

"Sorry," I said, my voice weary with exhaustion, "we just can't walk any faster."

"I'm not surprised," Dale said, glancing at my mod, super-tight dress slacks, "in those pants."

"Yeah, we're really wiped out," Teddy added.

"Okay, I get it," Dale snorted. "What, are you buckin' for more money? I told ya I can't give you a raise right now." He headed for his car. "See you next week."

Teddy and I shuffled along, casually monitoring Dale's departure. As he pulled out of the parking lot, we raised our arms to offer the limp wave of the cotton plantation slave, and then, under cover of darkness, jumped into the Firebird.

"Hurry," Teddy hollered, "before some loser from Kinney's sees the boxes!" Kinney's back door and Thom McAn's opened onto the same hallway, and they were our mortal enemies.

I lurched into the loading dock, throwing the car in park as Teddy raced up the stairs. He had stuck a small piece of cardboard in the door to keep it from locking, and he threw the door open as I shut the car motor off and switched off the headlights.

What felt like hours ticked by. No Teddy. This should have been a thirty-second operation. *Oh God*, I thought, panic rising inside me, *we shouldn't be doing this*. What were we thinking?

The temperature was below freezing, but sweat now stained my armpits. I began to hyperventilate, envisioning Teddy walking out with his hands in the air as a security guard held a gun to his head. I wondered if I'd be able to calm my serial-rapist prison roommate by playing "Muskrat Love" on my trumpet. I imagined standing at the Pearly Gates as Saint Peter read aloud the appalling list of transgressions I had committed, my friends and family gasping in horror at my malfeasance as Peter pushed the down button on the elevator.

Finally, the door opened, and Teddy sauntered slowly down the stairs, carrying the boxes as casually as possible.

"Hurry up!" I screamed inside the car. He strolled over to the dumpster and lifted the lid. Was he going to hide the evidence, I wondered? Had he, too, had a change of heart?

He dropped the lid of the dumpster and it banged shut with a BOOM. He was still holding the boxes. He raced over to the car. I threw open the door and he hurled the shoes into the backseat and jumped into the front.

"Go, GO!!"

I peeled out of the lot, headlights still off, tires screeching, Bonnie and Clyde before the bullets flew.

"What were you *doing*?" I screamed as I careened onto the plaza's main drag and into the parking lot of the nearby fast food restaurant where Teddy's car was stashed and where we would divvy up the loot.

"Some jerk from Kinney's walked out," he panted, referring to the loading dock hallway we shared. "I pretended like I was cleaning up the hallway. I told him I was just throwing out some empty boxes."

"Do you think he bought it?" I cried.

"I don't know!"

"Oh my God, oh my God, oh my God," I moaned. Sixteen years of nonthievery had, in one felonious moment, all gone up in smoke. I hoped prison stripes were horizontal—I was already tall enough.

• • •

"Oh my goodness!" Mother gasped, pulling the boots from the perfectly folded tissue inside the shoe box. "They're gorgeous!"

Until this moment, the holiday season had had all the whimsy of a cancer ward. The stress of the family's financial situation and Mother's unhappiness in her temp job had created an air of gloom. Mother's depression, it turned out, was far more painful to bear witness to than her tantrums, for I realized that one of the many things I loved about her was her strength.

Our gift exchange had been a meager one, the usual cavalcade of middle-class fabulosity reduced to simpler gifts of the socks and L'eggs panty hose variety.

But now, these stolen shoes were saving the day. Mother caressed the soft chocolate-brown leather. I could almost feel

Halston blessing the moment. *Joy to the world, the shoes have come.*

"Those are pretty cool," Val said, obviously impressed. "My taste has obviously worn off on you."

"I don't think," I replied haughtily, "that Kmart crop tops and a gallon of Charlie exactly make you Gloria Vanderbilt."

"How on earth did you afford them?" Mother gushed. "They must have cost you your whole salary."

"Oh, it was nothing," I replied nervously, noting the unfortunate irony of this statement.

She carefully pulled the knee-high boots on.

"Ray, zip me."

Dad galumphed over and bent down to zip up the boots. Mother's delight was, unfortunately, doing little to assuage my guilt. As I attempted to glow with the spirit of high style, I found myself longing, instead, to climb into a time machine.

Dad fiddled intently with the zipper. Thirty seconds passed.

"What are you doing down there?" Mother said, annoyed.

"The zipper's stuck," he grunted.

"Well, fix it."

"It won't move."

"Here," I said airily, kneeling down, "let me. I'm a professional." I pressed the sides of the zipper track together and yanked repeatedly on the tab. It wouldn't budge.

My fingers began to ache as I gritted my teeth. This stupid zipper was derailing the taste-making moment I had risked imprisonment to create.

I gave it one last, heroic yank. And the entire zipper came off in my hand.

"What?" Mother said, looking down at me.

The blood drained from my face as I held up the broken zipper. Val rolled her eyes and mouthed, "Way to go."

"Well, thank goodness you work there," Mother said with a sigh, patting my hand. "At least you can exchange them."

• • •

I paced around my bedroom, wondering where on earth I was gonna get the money to *buy* a pair of boots since I had no receipt to exchange the ones I'd stolen.

"We're out of your size," I lied to Mother, "but we'll be getting a new shipment of boots soon."

The next day, while Dale was taking a Parliament break in the stockroom, I shuffled up to him.

"Hey, um, can I ask you a favor?"

His face was dark. He suddenly seemed to be in a black mood. He stared at me and exhaled a series of impressive smoke rings. "I'm really not in the mood to be doing any favors for *you*." He leaned his head out the door to the sales floor. "Teddy, get in here!"

Teddy sauntered into the back room, then stopped in his tracks the moment he saw Dale's face. His smile faded. We glanced at each other nervously. Since that fateful night, neither of us had spoken of our crime. But had someone else? Moments earlier, Dale had been out front talking to the manager from Kinney's.

"Yes, sir?" Teddy said obsequiously. We never called Dale "sir."

Dale set his jaw. This could not be good.

"You guys are in deep shit."

Teddy and I stood frozen in place, staring straight ahead, afraid to breathe.

"You two have always been a problem for me," he continued, flicking his ash into a Styrofoam coffee cup. "A big, fat problem."

Dale knew. I was no longer Halston, just a Hood.

"You have given me nothing but grief since you started here."

We stood stiffly, awaiting the guillotine. *Please God*, I thought, *let it be mercifully swift.*

"But I really went to bat for you with the district manager." He smiled at us with the look of Queen Elizabeth bestowing a knighthood. "I got you an extra twenty-five cents an hour!"

Teddy and I looked at each other in shock. "What?"

"I was hoping for thirty-five cents, but you know, January's hell in retail—it's all returns." He puffed out his concave chest. "You're gettin' a raise!"

"Oh my God!" Teddy gasped with relief.

"That's… great," I replied, horrified.

Dale chuckled and elbowed me. "Really had you guys goin' there, didn't I?"

I had stolen from Thom McAn. And now, they were giving me a raise.

• • •

I began brown-bagging my work meals. I went cold turkey on leisure suits and Kools. Life was a dreary series of algebra tests, band rehearsals, and work shifts, with no visits to Jeans West or the Wild Pair to glam things up.

But after a long, desolate winter, my sacrifice paid off. By spring, I had saved up enough to purchase a new pair of boots.

I was fairly giddy with anticipation one March evening as I sat in the family room, waiting for the garage door opener to grind into action. I propped open the box containing Mother's new boots like a display case for the Hope diamond, rehearsing my *Price Is Right* prize flourish in order to direct everyone's attention.

Mother threw open the family room door.

"Good news!" she hollered as she marched in.

I smiled modestly. "Thanks. I double-checked the zipper on 'em and everything."

"I got," she said, oblivious to the brown beauties awaiting her, "a new job!"

"Oh," I said, quickly reclining in front of the box to mask its presence, sensing that her elation might render the boots unnecessary. "That's really cool!"

She suddenly stopped. She reached around me and picked up one of the boots.

"Well, *great*," she said in an exasperated tone. "They finally get these in when it's too warm to wear them. You tell those idiots at Thom McAn that I said…"

• • •

Two months later, I sent an anonymous note to Thom McAn headquarters.

"Dear Thom," I typed, so that the handwriting could not be identified later at trial, "I regret to inform you that I stole some shoes from you. Enclosed is payment. I'm so very sorry."

In the envelope was cash to cover the retail cost (having wisely determined that if I paid the employee-discounted price, they'd know I worked there) of Mother's boots.

I refused to pay the sales tax with my reimbursement, considering this their cross to bear since, if they hadn't made it so easy to steal, this never would have happened.

Chapter 4

NEW YORK STATE OF BLIND

The very notion of it conjured up images of creativity and chic urbanity. The Garment District. Park Avenue. Broadway. A city, I thought, where even the bums must wear Bill Blass. New York was the fashion capital of the world, and as a budding arbiter of taste and style, it was time for me to be a part of it.

This was, of course, easier said than done, given that it was 1979, and I was a college freshman working at a Fotomat film-developing kiosk in the parking lot of the Cross Keys shopping center, earning fifty cents over minimum wage dispensing glossy and matte-finish pictures to pervs who captured their soft-core exploits on film.

This astoundingly tedious job barely paid for the high-style clothes I required as a protégé (unbeknownst to him) of Halston. And in two and a half years since joining the workforce, I had only managed to save $1,200. But that would give me enough to afford a trip to the center of the sophistication universe, where I would soak up the lifestyle and haunts of my hero and find the inspiration for my own wildly successful career as a tastemaker—although it was not entirely clear to me what kind of taste I would be making, given that I had never been moved to sew a dress and could barely draw a stick figure to play Hangman.

Blowing all my savings for a trip to New York would give me the chance to define this goal. It was an investment in my fashion-forward future.

I would, of course, need a travel partner, someone who could take notes as inspirations sprang from my freshly stimulated imagination. The obvious choice was my girlfriend, Jenny, a clarinet player I had met in high school band. We had originally begun dating because I was friendly with her best friends, band members Nannette and Leslie, whom I regularly insulted with bon mots I developed by auditioning them into a Radio Shack cassette recorder at home.

Jenny didn't seem to mind that I was not, perhaps, regarded as the most virile or sports-minded member of the band. She accepted me just as I was, and I, in turn, accepted her shortcomings, which primarily consisted of a lack of commitment to the clarinet, a quality I tacitly encouraged, since, frankly, there could only be one star in the relationship.

She was a pretty, intelligent, freckle-faced girl with long blond hair and a chest that would not require augmentation in virtually any culture—a quality that seemed, at least to my brass-section cohorts, considerably more important than personality, musical ability, or, for that matter, having a head.

Jenny and I had spent most of our high school dating
life rubbing and grinding against one another, more or less
clothed, at romantic locales like the grassy knoll next to the
swing set at a local park. This activity had served as a surprisingly effective form of contraception. But as our skin
developed rug burns and the white-hot sparkle of bumping
uglies with our pants on began to dim, Jenny had decided to
go away to school, to a college 120 miles away.

And although she remained committed, the distance was
beginning to take its toll on our relationship. This trip to
New York, I was certain, was just what would bring us back
together. How better to express my love for her than by getting naked and greased up in a four-star Manhattan hotel?

It *was* love, right?

It certainly felt like love, although I really had nothing to
compare it to. I had loved many things in my lifetime—my
family, my guinea pigs, my platform shoes from Wild Pair—
but none of them had made me feel as good, as accepted, as
whole as Jenny. I had read somewhere that the best marriages
were comprised of people who were friends, and Jenny and
I were just that. We were great friends. Confidants. On the
same wavelength.

"What movie do you want to see?" I would ask.

"I'm dying to see *Ice Castles*."

"Oh my God, me, too!"

• • •

I decided to plan the trip with the help of my aunt and
uncle, theater artists who had been to New York many times,

and who understood what it meant to be creative. The black sheep of the family, they were, according to Mother and Dad, dangerous hippie liberals.

"They're *basically* good people," Mother said about her only brother and his wife when they wrote to tell us they were coming to visit. "But they'd just as soon we were all saluting Chairman Mao and fighting over bread."

"Just turn a deaf ear to their opinions," Dad warned me. He added with a wink, "You've got a leg up on this one."

They arrived one Saturday afternoon in their new car, a weird-looking Japanese brand called Toyota.

"I guess nobody told 'em," Dad whispered as they drove up, "that we beat the Japs in World War II."

I ran out to the car to greet them, smoothing my new Calvin Klein peasant shirt and coordinated pants. Halston was the architect of minimalist style, and I felt that Calvin—being the closest menswear designer to that aesthetic—might subliminally inspire my uncle, who clearly felt that clothes were a sort of wallpaper for the body. While he advised me about New York, I would advise him about personal panache.

"I'm so glad you came!" I gushed, leaning in the car window. "I'm heading to New York for a research trip and I figured you guys could give me some tips. Do you think I can get a good hotel for fifty dollars a night?" I smiled at them with a newly rehearsed air of fashion superiority. "I want something that befits my sense of style."

Uncle Stewart, a lanky, bespectacled man in his midforties—and the family's master of droll commentary—climbed out of the diminutive hatchback, omnipresent pipe in hand.

"Well," he replied, "Fifty dollars should buy you a hotel that you won't get murdered in."

"What?" I exclaimed, horrified.

Mother's side of the family rarely hugged, choosing meaningful glances over the intertwining of limbs, and Uncle Stewart was no different. He winked and raised his pipe.

Aunt Nancy, a pretty, petite woman in her late thirties, with flaming red hair and a penchant for maxi dresses and Birkenstocks, extricated herself from the passenger side, sipping oolong tea from a thermos. She had far less reservations about physical contact, and she hugged me immediately.

"My God, you're skin and bones. What is your mother feeding you?"

"Certainly not brown rice and tofu," Mother said, her teeth slightly gritted as she made a rare appearance in the front yard. Mother was very busy ironing underwear and making lists of cleaning duties for my father, and obviously felt that her public appearances should be reserved for coronations and the christening of naval destroyers.

"Ray, take their bags!" she barked at Dad, who, in his traditional tank-top undershirt, Sansabelt slacks, and moccasins, had clearly not overdressed for the occasion. He dutifully loaded himself down with their bags and staggered up the driveway.

"How great that Eric is going to visit the Big Apple," Aunt Nancy said as we walked into the house.

"I'm not sure why he wants to visit that cesspool of human misery," Mother replied, knowing full well that they were frequent visitors to the city. "Hopefully it'll teach him that there's no place like home."

"*Or* that there's a world outside of Yonkers," Aunt Nancy replied, quoting a song lyric from *Hello, Dolly*, a reference likely lost on everyone but me. I nodded sagely at her.

As Mother returned to her urgent laundry duties in the basement and Dad retired to his workbench—an effort to avoid awkward conversations since they had little in common with these Woodstock weirdos—I led Aunt Nancy and Uncle Stewart to the kitchen to continue our conversation.

"You know," Aunt Nancy said, somewhat tentatively as she curled her legs underneath her in a kitchen chair, "we have an actor friend who lives in Manhattan who would probably let you stay with him for a few days."

"Oh, thanks," I said quickly, "but…"

"Now," she whispered, glancing at me out of the corner of her eye, "Joel is *gay*. Would that bother you?"

"Well, of course it wouldn't bother me," I replied, wondering why she would choose to introduce me to someone of the homosexual persuasion. This would horrify Mother and Dad, but as a young sophisticate, I considered myself more open-minded. "Love the sinner, hate the sin," I said, parroting the words of our bomb-throwing reel-to-reel minister, B. R. Tibbits.

I had to admit, staying with a gay actor sounded terribly exotic and colorful, like rooming with a circus freak. For a brief moment, I debated jettisoning Jenny, since two guests would clearly be an imposition on Joel. But Jenny was too excited about the trip to cancel now.

I leaned in, also whispering so that Mother and Dad wouldn't hear. "Thanks for the offer, but Jenny's going with me. Don't tell Mother and Dad."

"Oh, so you're still dating *her*," Aunt Nancy replied, an odd disappointment coloring her voice.

"Yep," I replied proudly. "Two and a half years, can you believe it?"

"Not really," Uncle Stewart replied.

Aunt Nancy scribbled a phone number on a piece of paper. "Here's Joel's number. Just in case," she said with an oddly hopeful smile.

I dutifully stuffed it into my pocket as they began to pepper me with suggestions on attending big, boring museums and experimental theater so far off Broadway it might as well have been in New Jersey.

"There are some good youth hostels around the Bowery," Nancy suggested, "if you want to save some money on accommodations. I mean, there's so much to do in New York, you won't be spending a lot of time in your room."

"Thanks," I replied, trying not to let disappointment color *my* voice, "but I'm really more of a *swanky* hotel, museum *gift shop*, and *Broadway* theater guy." It was becoming all too clear by their Communist-unchic tips that we were of different minds. This was my first trip on my own, and my first to New York. I had to do it Halston style. After all, deprivation did not provoke inspiration.

• • •

Jenny and I arrived in Manhattan on a beautiful spring evening.

"Wow, it's so... dirty," she said, clinging to me as the cab crawled through the sex shops and discount electronics stores of Times Square.

"But exciting, isn't it?" I said as I fingered the collar of my black turtleneck—Halston's trademark look—and gazed out at the streets that had produced a towering tastemaker like him. "I mean, look, the Barrymore Theatre. The *Brooks Atkinson*." I had no idea who Brooks Atkinson was, but who cared, his name was on a theater. These city streets were awash in culture. I couldn't wait to be creatively inspired.

"It seems a little dangerous," she whispered.

I smiled. Once we were ensconced in our room at the dazzling Sheraton Centre Hotel—a room that cost *seventy-nine* dollars a night—she would feel differently. Especially since I had determined that tonight, our first night in the land of Halston, would be the night of our romantic coupling.

And indeed, when I opened the door to our room on the thirty-fifth floor a half hour later, Jenny gasped with delight.

"Oh, how beautiful!" She dropped her bag and rushed to the window.

"A beautiful view for a beautiful girl," I said masterfully, relieved that we didn't look into a porno theater or a brick wall, which my uncle had warned me about. I opened one of the large windows (suitable for jumping out of) and discreetly pulled out the cassette tape recorder that I had packed. As I switched on the perfectly cued-up *A Star Is Born* soundtrack, Barbra Streisand's voice blared from the tiny speaker, the cassette somewhat distorted from overuse, and the opening strains of "Evergreen" began to play.

Jenny sat in the windowsill, awestruck at the carpet of lights provided by the skyscrapers of midtown Manhattan, as I switched off one of the two bedside lamps and quietly withdrew a baggie full of rose petals to sprinkle across the bed. Since the rosebushes in our yard in St. Louis were not yet in bloom, the petals were dried, but the effect, I felt, was equally as stylish.

"Why are you tossing potpourri on the bed?"

"It's aromatic!" I replied defensively. "It's romantic."

Jenny crossed her arms nervously, obviously aware of my intentions although we had not entirely discussed the matter. "Did you get rubbers?"

Before we left St. Louis, I had been so preoccupied with the stylistic elements of this moment that there had been little time to consider such practicalities as birth control.

"No, I kinda figured *you* would get 'em."

"Now, why would *I* buy rubbers?" she snapped. "How would that make me look?"

The next hour was spent in a frantic crosstown search for a gas station or diner bathroom whose condom machine wasn't empty. We quickly found ourselves less than enchanted at the parade of dingy, cockroach-infested storefronts of Seventh Avenue, but I refused to remove any rose-colored glasses I might currently be wearing.

"New York smells," Jenny said, wrinkling her nose.

"That's the smell of *life*," I replied enthusiastically. "It's gritty. It's real. It's raw."

"Well, it's kinda gross."

I sighed. Granted, I wanted to take a bottle of Windex to the entire city, but how could she not see the beauty and excitement of this pulsating center of the creative universe?

"There's a drugstore by our hotel," Jenny said finally, weary of standing in the doorways of these seedy establishments like a nervous gun moll. "Is there a reason we couldn't just go there?"

It had somehow not occurred to me that, since we were in another city entirely, no one would know who I was, so there was little need for secrecy. We rushed back to the fluorescent-lit safety of Duane Reade, where, always thinking ahead,

I purchased *two* rubbers, figuring that my lovemaking would be so masterful that an encore would be virtually assured. Since that fateful night with Kathy a couple of years earlier, I had spent much time alone in my bedroom, practicing my moves—and was reasonably certain that this time, there would be no fumbling, no Marlin Perkins moments, no vomiting.

There would, however, be wine, which I had discreetly packed into my seventy-pound suitcase. Boone's Farm Strawberry Hill, a complex varietal with top notes of 7Up and grape Kool-Aid that would give the evening just the elegant touch it needed. So as not to distract her with a lot of labored sipping and awkward conversation, I downed three-quarters of the bottle while Jenny was in the bathroom, and by the time she returned wearing a pink satin nightie, I was Ricardo Montalban welcoming her to Fantasy Island.

"Don't the lights make a beautiful backdrop?" I said, doing a *Price Is Right* arm sweep as she crossed the room and sat on the bed. The rose petals crunched, creating a dreamy sound as though we were walking through the forest. The forest, I thought, of our love.

"Oww!"

"Oh, sorry," I said, pulling a shard from underneath her. "Pinecone."

I leaned over and kissed her, and we began to make out. Jenny had, unfortunately, taken so long in the bathroom that, although I had rewound the cassette twice, the *Star Is Born* soundtrack had moved on from "Evergreen" and was now on "The Woman in the Moon," the show-stopping song that makes Streisand's character a star.

"Ummm," Jenny said tentatively as she grabbed my arms, "can you not do the hand motions?"

I discovered that the alcohol was providing a quite singular focus—one that did not, unfortunately, include practical knowledge of prophylactics. And as we removed our clothes, I realized that I had no idea how to don this latex love killer. I sat on the edge of the bed, trying to read the wrapper in the dim light of the one lit lamp.

"What's wrong?"

"It looks awfully narrow," I said, holding up the condom. "Is it supposed to cut off the circulation?"

"I don't know," she replied, pulling the sheet up to her chest. "Maybe that's so it'll stay on."

"Well, do I just put it on the top, like a beret?"

Jenny leaned over, staring at my crotch with all the wanton carnality of Margaret Mead, which mortified me—she didn't really need to see my private parts up close.

"There's too much plastic for that. I think it's supposed to go all the way down."

"Well," I replied testily, "do I unroll it first and then put it on, or vice versa?"

"Does it say on the wrapper?"

I eventually succeeded in putting it on inside out, whereupon it rolled up and came off inside Jenny's vagina.

• • •

Our second attempt at lovemaking went a bit more smoothly, and we finally collapsed into a heap of sweaty, tangled limbs.

I lay there for what felt like an appropriate amount of time (forty-five seconds), and then politely excused myself.

"Where are you going?" Jenny said as I leaped out of bed and galloped to the bathroom.

"Oh, just gonna rinse off," I replied in as bright a tone as I could muster.

As I stood under the scalding-hot shower for twenty minutes, scrubbing my groin region until it was red and puffy, I wondered if I would need to do this every night we were in New York.

Oh, it had been fun, sort of. And most importantly, Jenny seemed to enjoy it, and that made me supremely happy. My band friend Leslie had once told me that this sort of thing really cemented a couple, and that had seemed like a good reason to do it.

At the time.

I awoke the next morning, my head foggy and pounding slightly, to find Jenny gazing at me with a soft smile.

I sat up quickly, annoyed.

"What?" I snapped. No one ever saw me this unkempt, and I didn't appreciate being inspected like a nearly expired rump roast.

"Oh, nothing," she replied, a bit taken aback. "You just looked so…" She turned to face the ceiling.

I immediately regretted my loutishness.

"So, what are we doing today?" she said meekly.

"Today," I said grandly, trying to warm the chill I had cast over the room, "I'm showing you the *real* New York."

We set off on a glamorous Gray Line bus tour that drove us by New York's most hallowed cultural institutions at forty miles an hour. The Plaza Hotel. Macy's flagship store. The hottest nightclub on the planet, Studio 54. And ground zero for New York sophistication, Roy "Halston" Frowick's town house. As I stared dreamily at the dark glass of the four-story building on East 63rd Street, Jenny turned to me.

"Why do you care so much about a clothing designer?"

I suddenly realized that I had never voiced my dream of becoming a tastemaker aloud. For all she knew, I was still hell-bent on becoming the trumpet-playing Barry Manilow.

"Well," I stammered, "he's inspiring."

"Sure, I guess," she replied. "If you're a designer." She paused. "That's not what you want to *be*, is it?"

I stared out the bus window mutely. Her tone implied that this would be a slightly ridiculous career choice. I didn't have the courage to ask if it was absurd because she thought I had no talent, or if she thought it was somehow less than masculine.

Was it a crazy idea?

We spent the afternoon touring the shops of Rockefeller Plaza and Fifth Avenue, Jenny's arm in mine, as I soaked up the opulence of New York's most fashionable stores: Bonwit Teller. Bergdorf Goodman. Gucci. Jenny loved shopping and was happy to wander through these shrines to style, although her practical nature was rapidly interfering with my creative inspiration.

"Seriously?" she said wryly, holding up a cashmere sweater that had been marked down to $145. "Who *pays* this?"

"You can't put a price on quality," I replied with a touch of disdain.

"Sure you can," she said, unfazed. "I'd say about sixty dollars."

"Well," I replied huffily, "it's also about the shopping experience."

"Screw the experience," she replied. "You can't wear the experience."

I sighed. Granted, we were both broke college students, but I, for one, understood the psychological importance of luxury.

"Let's go to Saks," I said, using the sophisticated shortened name for the gold standard of department stores, Saks Fifth Avenue, as I walked a step or two ahead of her to avoid the now constant intertwining of her arm with mine. "I need to pick up a little Halston."

"Isn't Halston a women's designer?" she hollered from behind me.

"Of course," I replied authoritatively. "But he's entered the fragrance arena for men."

Could I design a cologne? I wondered silently as we entered the stately, ornate building. What were my favorite smells?

I thought for a moment. Lemon Pledge. Comet. Bacon.

We approached a good-looking young salesman behind the perfume counter, whose name tag said Jonathon.

"Good afternoon," he said with a smile, locking eyes with me as though Jenny wasn't there.

"Hi," I said in what, to my surprise, turned out to be a deeper, sexier tone than I usually used. Jenny sort of chuckled oddly in the background. "I'd like to try the 1-12 and Z-14."

"Of course." As Jonathon ceremoniously handed me the first bottle of Halston cologne, our fingers touched for a moment and a sort of electricity shot through me. *You certainly have to be good-looking to work here*, I thought. *All the men here are so handsome.*

All the men and women.

"The bottle was designed by Elsa Peretti," he said to me, still apparently unaware that Jenny was present. The colognes came in voluptuous bottles carved, I now realized, from the same smoky-brown glass as Halston's town house. For a brief moment, I envisioned Jonathon and I having cocktails with Halston and Liza in the living room of his trendy home, laughing uproariously as Liza told another hilarious story about life with Judy Garland.

This is the kind of person I need to be around, I thought. *He inspires me.*

"Who's Elsa Peretti?" Jenny asked inquisitively, startling Jonathon with her sudden presence, and reminding me that she was there. I stepped out of Jenny's line of sight and rolled my eyes knowingly to Jonathon. I had no idea, either, but at least I was classy enough not to ask.

"A jewelry designer," Jonathon said, dabbing a bit of cologne onto his finger. "May I?" He touched my neck lightly.

Electricity again. Jenny glanced at me curiously.

"Uh, I'll take it," I said quickly, handing him the Z-14.

"That'll be thirty-two dollars."

In a normal setting, I'd have swallowed my tongue. Thirty-two dollars was an entire day's work. For a single small bottle of cologne. But I was lost in the moment. There, in Halston's living room, Liza was starting to sing.

I handed Jonathon forty dollars. "Keep the change," I said grandly.

"Thank you," Jonathon replied with a smile, handing me a shopping bag and some money, "but we're not allowed to accept tips."

Jenny grabbed my arm with a bit more force than seemed necessary and led me toward the door. As I carried the glitzy Saks shopping bag for all the world to see, I dreamily envisioned a life with friends like Halston and Liza. And Jonathon.

As we reached the front of the store, where a display of Halston colognes stood welcoming shoppers, I held the door open for two middle-aged women swathed in diamonds and mink coats.

"Can you believe," one woman said to the other as they marched in with nary an acknowledgment of my gentlemanly kindness, "that Halston is hawking cologne now?"

Her friend clucked her tongue. "He's one step," she replied, "from going J.C. Penney."

They both laughed.

• • •

That night, we sat at the elegant Four Seasons restaurant in the Seagram building, having a prix-fixe dinner so expensive I wondered if it came with closing papers. I had saved up for events like this as a way to commemorate the rekindling of our relationship.

But all I could focus on was the words of those women in Saks. Was the man I so admired over? Was I a fool for wanting to emulate him?

I wanted desperately to take in Jenny's awe at the gorgeous decor, the celebrity clientele, the supremely snotty waitstaff. But I could only wonder: *Do I really have any taste? Do I have any future in the world of style?*

An hour later, as we walked to the Imperial Theatre for the next stop on my itinerary of creative fabulosity, Jenny reached for my hand.

"Is something wrong?" she asked. "You've been kind of in your own world all day."

"I'm sorry," I said as I gazed into her bright-blue eyes. "I'm just a little overwhelmed."

"Me, too," she whispered. "People here are so *rude*."

The Broadway show *They're Playing Our Song* was a smash hit musical that starred Lucie Arnaz and Robert Klein. And at 10:30, as the curtain rang down, my hands bloodred and my hair now plastered to my sweaty face from the exertion of my effusive clapping, an answer to my question had begun to form.

I had always loved music. I had played in the orchestras of two high school musicals. I had sung in the concert choir. I *had* musical talent. Granted, I had never set foot on a real stage, but if the comedian Robert Klein—who had pretty much zero musical ability—could become a Broadway star, what was stopping *me*?

When we returned to the hotel, I deposited Jenny in the elevator.

"Where are you going?"

"I'm too amped up," I replied. "It's this New York City rhythm," I said, quoting Barry Manilow. "I'm gonna go for a walk."

I wandered the mean streets of New York for nearly an hour, mentally mapping out the exciting new future that now lay before me.

Screw tastemaking and style, I thought. I would become famous the old-fashioned way—by singing and dancing my way into America's hearts.

Although I had no idea if I actually possessed talent as a theatrical performer, I had been, I reminded myself, a trumpet semistar. I had performed with my high school's concert choir. I had played in the orchestra of the school's musicals and carefully evaluated my classmates as they lumbered across the stage. Was it such a stretch to think that I could become Broadway's one singular sensation?

I fingered the slip of paper that I had carried in my pocket since leaving St. Louis. On it was written my aunt and uncle's friend Joel's number. *I really should call him*, I thought. Gay or not, now that I was pursuing a career in the theater, he'd be a good contact.

But it was late.

By the time I returned, beautiful Jenny was, to my relief, asleep.

• • •

The next day, I amended my carefully planned itinerary to make time for a walking tour of the theater district. As we wandered from venue to venue, dodging heroin addicts and hobos, me snapping countless pictures of the marquees with my 110 Instamatic with built-in flash, I imagined the flash of paparazzi cameras as I stood at the stage door of a Broadway theater, signing autographs for screaming fans who heaved their (hopefully laundered) underwear at my face.

"I don't know what half of these shows are," Jenny said, a bit bored, as I oohed and ahhed over yet another marquee.

A group of ridiculously good-looking chorus boys passed us, laughing and carrying on, as they sauntered toward the rear of the Broadhurst Theatre. I quickly pointed my Instamatic and snapped.

"Why are you taking a picture of guys walking into a theater?" Jenny said, mystified.

"It's an atmospheric shot!" I snapped. "That's the stage door." I crossed to the box office and stared at the one-sheet for the show. "Ooh. We should get tickets for this. It's directed by Bob Fosse."

"Who's Bob Fosse?"

"I won't even dignify that with an answer."

"Is it just dancing, or is there other stuff?"

"I don't know. Why does it matter? Let's just be spontaneous!" I said, exhilarated.

"You hate spontaneity."

• • •

That night, in a final effort to give Jenny the fullest experience of New York glamour, I had booked us a table at Broadway's most famous boîte, Sardi's.

"Look, Carol Channing!" I exclaimed in a whisper. "Angela Lansbury!"

"Uh-huh."

I gazed in rapture at the caricatures lining the walls as we sat at a cramped table by the kitchen, grazing on overpriced entrées that had required *many* diligent hours of ransacking Fotomat customers' snapshots in search of nudie pics. But it was worth it for Jenny to get to experience all that New York—which held in its filthy hands my sparkling new future—had to offer. One day, I thought, we might sit under my caricature on this very wall.

"Penny for your thoughts," Jenny said with a hopeful smile. "Or, in this city," she added, "a quarter. Man, is it expensive here."

It won't seem like that for long, I thought. *When I sweep into Sardi's after my triumphant, Tony-winning debut in the smash hit musical of the season, producers will be throwing money at the floor to provide a carpet for my talented feet.*

How had Broadway stardom never occurred to me before, I wondered? My mother, who for years had had Lady Macbeth moments over something as simple as Dad defrosting the wrong casserole for dinner, had always possessed a flair for the dramatic. Surely I had inherited that.

"I'm just excited to see the dancers."

"Yeah," Jenny replied, a slight note of resignation in her voice, "that's what I thought."

Bob Fosse's *Dancin'* was a giant musical hit—a multi-act orgy of top hats and slutty dance moves that left me breathless.

"That was incredible," I gasped as we walked out to the street to hail a cab.

"Yes," she replied, a tad less emphatic than I. "It was very nice. Although not much in the plot department."

"It's a revue!" I snapped with exasperation. "Do you know what that *is*?"

Her freckled face turned a deep shade of red. "Why are you getting so mad? I liked it, I just—"

"This is art!" I hollered. "Culture. I appreciate these things. And apparently, you don't."

A gloomy silence hung over the cab ride back to the hotel as I pondered my truculent behavior.

"Penny for *your* thoughts," I said brightly, trying to lighten the mood.

She said nothing for a moment and just stared out the window at a body being fished out of a dumpster. When she finally spoke, her voice cracked a bit.

"We're not really a match anymore, are we?"

"Well, sure we are," I said, somewhat panicked at the implication of her words, even if I recognized a certain amount of truth in them. "We both love Barry Manilow, and mood rings, and Broadway shows…"

"No, *you* like Broadway shows," she replied. "And I like being with *you*. But you're… changing."

"No, I'm not," I said. "I'm still the same outrageously handsome, extraordinarily humble guy you've always known."

She didn't smile. "You're changing."

"Well," I said, becoming defensive, "I can't help it that my world is expanding."

She turned and gazed at me for a moment. "No," she said quietly. "You can't."

I did not attempt to re-create any scenes from *A Star Is Born* that night—including the one with Streisand and Kristofferson in the bathtub surrounded by votive candles (which I had conveniently packed, along with enough matches to torch the airplane). Like Esther and John Norman, we loved each other. But not, it seemed, enough.

• • •

A few weeks later, Jenny broke up with me for good. I had not told her of my new career choice. But she had nonetheless decided that we were simply on different paths.

And in my heart, I knew she was right. With any luck, I would be going on to fame and fortune as a beloved icon of the American musical theater. And she clearly didn't like New York. It could never work.

But it was sad. We had invested nearly three of the best years of our lives in one another. The loss of this wonderful, supportive girl—who had opened the door to sweet, Barry White–style lovemaking—was heartbreaking.

But I will go on, I decided bravely. *I will make it through. And somehow, I will turn this tragedy into a triumph.*

And then it came to me.

I'll invite her to my Broadway opening.
That'll make her regret it.

···· Chapter 5 ····

TUNE DEAF

My identity began to crystallize fully when I performed the Barbra Streisand song "On a Clear Day."

As a lounge number.

With jazz hands.

Since my trip to New York a few months earlier, I had become consumed with Broadway musicals. *Evita. Sweeney Todd.* And my personal favorite, *The Best Little Chicken Ranch in Texas* (the title used to advertise it in St. Louis, where whores don't exist), which was directed and choreographed by the man I had decided to impersonate.

Emulate.

Tommy Tune was an extraordinary talent from a modest background. He was from the heartland of America. And he was now the hottest director/choreographer in show business. Although at nineteen I was not yet sure of the extent of my own gifts as an actor/singer/dancer, Tommy and I shared the same background and love for the theater. These commonalities—along with my musical aptitude and desperate desire to be seen—were enough to convince me of my destiny. Surely, all the creative detours I had taken were merely part of the path that had led me to this moment.

Tommy began his career as a thespian, so the most efficient way to begin getting *my* name on everyone's lips, I logically surmised, would be to star in a local show. This interim, pre-Broadway step also seemed appropriate given that I had never actually set foot on a stage.

I began my new career with tap-dancing instruction from an eminent local director, Debra Kingston, who gave group lessons in her basement for six bucks a pop. As a theater professor at Florissant Valley Community College, Debra presided over semiannual musical productions where some of North St. Louis County's finest talents who couldn't get into a four-year university trundled across the stage in search of transferable credit.

Tommy would be proud, I thought, as I executed a tap combination in Debra's basement with what I felt was a catlike grace, born of the thousands of nights I had spent creeping stealthily around the house to avoid Mother's ire.

"No, no, *no!*" Debra hollered, putting her face in her hands.

It was 1980, and I had just seen *Fame*. So I knew how mercurial theatrical personalities could be in the pursuit of molding their students' talent. And it was thus with fortitude that I accepted Debra's criticism of my tap dancing. No artistic endeavor worth its salt came easy, but with pluck and dedication and Debra's screaming, I would become the Great White Gregory Hines.

Six weeks into these lessons, she took me aside.

"You have a nice singing voice," she said gently. "Why don't we focus on that?"

Did I suck? Or had I mastered this form of dance with an ease that indicated a wellspring of talent bubbling up to the surface? Surely Debra's desire to move me into another area of training this soon was a good omen. Stardom was calling my name. At least, I think that was the case; it was hard to be sure with just one good ear.

● ● ●

My parents were less enthused about my new interest.

"You know we've always supported your creative endeavors," Mother began, her voice muffled as she Ajaxed the inside of the self-cleaning oven. "Even the stupid ones." Dad handed her a fresh can of cleanser. "You certainly have musical talent, but you shouldn't be wasting it in the theater—it's filled with liberals and godless heathens."

"And how are you gonna make a living doing theater in St. Louis?" Dad added. "Those mimes in front of the Arch make lousy tips."

I couldn't blame these talent-free troglodytes, of course. They had no frame of reference. As nine-to-five office drones, Mother and Dad couldn't possibly understand the inner whisper of creativity.

After nearly two months of voice lessons standing next to the spinet in Debra's living room, I was, I decided, ready for my close-up. My friend Candace, with whom I commuted to the University of Missouri, St. Louis, where we were laboring as sophomores, informed me of auditions for the theater department's musical *The Pajama Game*, and we began plotting our conquest of the stage.

"What song are you gonna sing?" I queried as we climbed into her car and I twisted the rearview mirror to check my hair.

"I'm gonna do 'The Rose,'" she said, snatching the rearview mirror back and placing big Jackie O sunglasses on top of her regular eyeglasses.

"No, you can't!" I cried. "*I'm* doing a ballad. I've been rehearsing 'Hard Candy Christmas' for weeks!"

"It's the only song I can sing a cappella," she snapped. "Besides, what do you care? We're not going up for the same roles." She paused. "Are we?"

"Oh, forget it," I replied. "I'll do an up-tempo number, then, and we'll just *see* who dazzles 'em."

The inspiration to reimagine "On a Clear Day" came several days later. And whether it was the snappy swing pacing or the white gloves on my hands, my artistic choices coalesced, I thought, into a performance that—for someone so new to the theatrical arts—positively sparkled.

I was certain the director saw potential in me; when I finished, he said to me with a certain indefinable awe, "Was that for real?"

The next afternoon, Candace and I and dozens of other auditionees swarmed around the cast list that had been posted outside the theater.

"I can't look," I said breathlessly. "Read it to me."

"The leads are…" Candace said excitedly as I closed my eyes and imagined Tommy Tune calling my name from the stage of the Tony awards as the audience erupted in foot-stomping cheers, "Gary Gilroy and Michelle O'Malley. Well, no surprise there. They're the Lunt and Fontanne of UMSL. But we got roles!" she announced brightly. "You're Factory Worker #3!"

As I stood in the lobby, elated at having been cast but somewhat crushed that my role was essentially high kicks and harmonies, I heard a voice whispering in my ear—a voice that must have been, based on the Texas accent, Tommy Tune's. "Okay, technically, it's a chorus part, but Eric, without the chorus, what would a musical be?" he said comfortingly. "Nothing more than a series of show-stopping solos. The chorus numbers provide a much-needed break during which the audience can talk loudly among themselves or go to the bathroom."

Tommy had just been nominated for his *second* Tony. And he had started in the chorus. Perhaps it was, I thought, a dues-paying exercise necessary to make the taste of stardom that much sweeter, to make that moment—when Tommy and I sit together in his New York penthouse, toasting our mutual Tony awards and reminiscing about my meteoric rise to fame—immensely more satisfying.

I decided to put my nose to the theatrical grindstone. And indeed, as rehearsals for *The Pajama Game* commenced, I seemed to be making real progress toward the theatrical fame that I felt would define me. Because the show, I discovered, was helping me to flower not only professionally, but personally.

For starters, there were a lot of women. Almost no one discussed sports. And as someone who had always suffered a dearth of male friends, I was thrilled by my blossoming friendship with another chorus member, Kurt, a blond, slightly overweight boy with whom I shared many interests, not the least of which was the show's twenty-three-year-old choreographer, Phillip.

It wasn't Phillip himself that Kurt and I were interested in, of course, since that would be weird. It was Phillip's coolness, his effortless ability to be both magnetic and aloof, to wear leg warmers *and* be masculine. Phillip looked like a model, with curly brown hair and charm to burn, and he moved with the utter self-assurance of a *Solid Gold* dancer.

Kurt and I would watch him, fascinated, as we vainly attempted to mimic his behavior. This was particularly challenging for Kurt, whose personality (which was on high beam at all times and blinded everyone in his path) left little room for accommodation. But as Kurt and I got to know one another better, I found myself drawn to his fearlessness, even if it didn't have the same effect as Phillip's. Kurt would talk to anyone and say anything. He was my childhood role model Endora, without the magic but *with* the moxie.

Our friendship was sealed when we attended a party at the home shared by Phillip and the star of the show, Gary, who was from a wealthy family. Gary owned a nine-thousand-square-foot mansion in the Central West End of St. Louis, a slightly shabby area of once-grand homes that were slowly being rediscovered. The entire cast had been invited to this party, but when we arrived, we were dismayed to discover that it also included many movers and shakers from the St. Louis arts community. These old farts (some well into their thirties) stood about, martinis in hand, lending a pompous air to the proceedings. Most of us had expected pizza, beer and Twister, but white-shirted waiters circulated with hors d'oeuvres and drinks as Gershwin emanated from the stereo. It was alternately fabulous and boring as hell.

Kurt and I whiled away much of the evening studying Phillip, as he flirted with the female cast members.

"*You*," Phillip said in a raspy whisper to Judy, the chunky, pretty girl who was my dance partner, "move like a much slimmer woman."

She almost fainted.

"He's so dreamy," she whispered as she floated off to the bar in search of an Annie Green Springs.

"It's like he has some sort of power," Kurt whispered as he smoothed his feathered hair, "that people are helpless to defend against."

Several hours (and screwdrivers) later, Kurt and I stood at the top of the home's grand staircase, no longer dazzled by the stultifying pretentiousness of the party below.

"We gotta liven this thing up," Kurt announced. "These people have sticks so far up their asses they're spitting up splinters."

He pointed to the mansion's coolest feature: a motorized chair, left by the elderly former owner, designed to carry her from the top of the staircase to the bottom.

"No," I said, reading his mind, "you can't!"

Seconds later, the motorized chair began to whir. "Light the candlllles!" Kurt bellowed in a brassy voice as he began to sing the famous number from the musical *Mame*. The chair began a painfully slow descent, with him in it. "Get the ice ouuuut!" He appeared to be channeling Ethel Merman.

The crowd below stopped talking and turned, as one, to the staircase.

"Roll the ruuuug up!"

Jaws dropped. Murmurs of "Good God!" and "What the hell?" crisscrossed the room.

The party came to a screeching halt as the chair arrived at the bottom. "It's todaaaay!"

A stony silence greeted his big finish. Kurt stepped out of the chair and, completely unfazed, barked, "Auntie Mame needs a cocktail!"

I was horrified by his lack of boundaries. I was *not* one to make a scene, and Kurt seemed to not only relish it, but to be virtually oblivious to the consequences. But we became inseparable from that moment on, attending the show's after-parties at the local dive bar together (though, curiously, never another one at Gary's house) and furtively discussing the difficulties of throwing around our female dance partners on stage.

"I'm gonna have to start lifting weights," I huffed as we practiced our steps in the lobby of the theater, "or Judy is gonna snap me like a twig." At six three and 150 pounds, I was essentially a walking wishbone. "But I don't mind. I'm sure Tommy started this way."

"Tommy who?"

"*Tune*," I replied. "Who else?"

"Hmm," Kurt replied. "Well, you two are a lot alike. You're both stupidly tall."

One night the following week, when Kurt had a late shift slinging biscuits at Church's Fried Chicken, I decided to go stag to the after-party, since I now felt such kinship with my fellow thespians.

As various castmates played pool and flirted, I stood watching Phillip play Space Invaders on the arcade machine twenty feet away. *I really should get to know him better*, I thought. Tommy Tune choreographs, and God willing, I, too, would one day be called upon to create dance magic. Summoning my courage, I sidled over to him as casually as I could manage.

"Bum a cigarette?"

He turned and stared at me for a moment, the full force of his charisma turned upon me. A flicker of a smile played across his lips. He pulled out a pack of Marlboros.

"Sure. Didn't know you smoked."

"Only when I drink," I said in a strangely husky voice that I only later recognized as my own, "so I smoke a *lot*."

He chuckled.

The bar we frequented didn't require fake IDs—they served underage drinkers as a badge of honor—and as my third dollar beer completed its sightseeing tour of my bladder, and "Call Me" by Blondie blared over the bar's jukebox, I excused myself and stepped into the tiny one-man men's room.

Mother would be appalled, I thought, as I unraveled several yards of toilet paper and placed it on the floor to protect my shoes.

As I began to pee, I heard the door open behind me. I turned to find Phillip squeezing into the confined space. Phillip, like all beautiful people, was not someone you kept waiting, so I hurried to finish. As I was leaning over to flush, I heard a clicking sound, and glanced back to see Phillip turning the lock.

Well, that's odd, I thought. If he needed privacy, wouldn't he prefer I be on the other side of the door? I turned to wash my hands, and as I did, Phillip grabbed my shoulders and whirled me around to face him. Before I knew what was happening, he kissed me.

I was completely taken aback. Granted, I, like everyone else in the cast, had admired his choreography, his cockiness, his curly hair. But it had never, in a million years, occurred to me that he might be admiring *me*.

Suddenly, a frat guy pounded on the door and announced, in a God-help-us-all-if-I-get-behind-the-wheel-tonight slur, that if I didn't hurry up, he was gonna pee on the pool table. Phillip threw open the door and brushed past the guy, leaving me standing in the bathroom, the toilet paper under my tennies askew, trying to assess what had just happened.

As I drove home, my mind reeled. I had been elected to the court of King Phillip! But at what price? The Reverend B. R. Tibbits had some choice words about men lying with other men, which included "hellfire," "eternal damnation," and "grossing God out."

• • •

I said nothing to Kurt or anyone else during the three-day weekend while *The Pajama Game* was on hiatus. Val, the only family member I could have even considered confiding in, had managed to get hitched to her policeman boyfriend some months earlier and now, as a cop's wife, was consumed by the glamour and status of not having to obey stop signs.

And as Reverend B. R. shouted warnings from the living room stereo about those who chose to indulge in such perversions of nature—"For every right man, there is only one right woman"—I had no one to turn to but the entity who was, apparently, judging me.

"It's not like I'm a homo or anything," I prayed. "I was just so thrilled to have someone cool actually like me. You know how that is," I said, gazing heavenward. "You must get it all the time."

Silence. No bolt of lightning cut the house in half, but there was also no conveyance of understanding, or acceptance.

I momentarily longed for the magical old bedspread of my youth. That tattered piece of chenille had helped me to cope with situations that felt out of my control. It had given me a sense of security when there was none, a feeling that I had some small measure of power over my life and circumstance.

But I had long ago lost track of it, assuming it had been donated to the Disabled Veterans in one of Mother's every-thing-goes clearance crazes. (I imagined a grizzled World War II vet now stroking the soft, tattered material, asking God for a Betty Grable pinup or some Nazis to strafe.)

And really, what did it matter? I was nineteen years old, far too mature to be looking outside myself for answers.

• • •

What would Tommy Tune think about this, I wondered as we returned to rehearsals. Tommy had not rocketed to stardom by indulging in such sinful, reckless behavior. In interviews, he always discussed the show he was working on, not his personal life. The best course of action, it seemed clear, would be to avoid Phillip at all costs and focus on my character. Discovering the motivation for Factory Worker #3 would require a lot of deep inner work, and I could not be distracted by a demon in Danskins.

One afternoon, as Kurt and I rehearsed a move where I had to balance Judy on my hip, Phillip passed by.

"No," he said patiently, grabbing my hips, his body pressed up against mine, "like this." He executed the move in a stylish yet load-bearing fashion as my body more or less followed suit. "That's better." He smiled his megawatt smile and sidled off to the bathroom as my legs almost buckled underneath me. Kurt stared at me curiously, his hands on his hips.

"Well, aren't *you* the teacher's pet. You know," he whispered, glancing around, "I heard a rumor that he's *gay*."

"Well, that's—that's ridiculous," I stammered. "Why would anybody think that?"

"I don't know if it's true or not, but you'd better watch yourself, or he'll think you're, like, coming on to him."

"Well, I'm not."

"You're not what?"

"Gay. Or coming on to him. Take your pick."

"I didn't say *you* were gay," he replied. We repeated the series of dance steps. "Anyway, it's probably for the best."

"Why?"

"Well, Phillip's a fox." I glanced over at him, surprised by this overtly queer statement.

"A *fox*?"

"What?" he replied defensively. "You don't have to be gay to figure that out. He can get anybody. So, no offense, but I kinda doubt he'd pick *you*."

This candid evaluation of my lack of hotness stung.

Although I would have placed my studliness somewhere just south of Ron Howard's, I didn't need someone shoving the needle toward Jimmie Walker from *Good Times*. We continued our rehearsal as I stewed in silence at his remark. Finally, unable to stand it anymore, I pulled Kurt into a corner.

"If I tell you something," I whispered, knowing his passion for tableware, "you have to swear on your mother's china that you won't tell anybody."

"I swear," Kurt promised, practically salivating. "On the Lenox."

"Phillip likes me."

"What?"

"We made out in the john at the bar." Kurt's eyes widened as I realized the complicity inherent in this statement and immediately began to backpedal. "Well, he made out with *me*, I mean, I didn't—"

"In the john? You made out in the john? Oh my God, that is so low-rent it almost sounds true!"

● ● ●

Two weeks passed. Nothing more had happened with Phillip since that night at the bar, and although I was naturally relieved, I had to admit that he could be a valuable ally in my attempt to ascend to the throne of Tommy Tune. And to that end, it occurred to me that a more overt emulation of the style of Tommy Tune might remind Phillip of my star potential.

I decided to pair Capezio dance slippers—shoes that I had seen Tommy Tune wearing in a publicity photo—with a new, carefully rehearsed dancer's walk. This masterful stride—wherein I slithered across the floor with what I felt was a tigerlike sensuality—completed my transformation. Although it did cause Kurt to inquire if I'd had a stroke.

But none of this seemed to be garnering the attention of Phillip, so, at the next after-party a couple of nights later at the bar, I spent most of the evening waiting in the bathroom. Finally, at around eleven thirty, Phillip sidled in. He squeezed past me and began to pee as I washed my hands for the eleventh time.

"Why is everything covered in toilet paper?"

"Oh, yeah, I noticed that, too. Weird, huh."

"God," he said, a note of exasperation in his voice, "Gary is such a dick."

"Why?" I said, excited to be sharing gossip about the star of the show. "What did he do?"

"He thinks that because he got me this gig he can order me around."

"Well," I replied, "he is the Lunten Fontanne of St. Louis."

"Those are two different people."

"Oh."

Phillip zipped up and turned to me.

"I wish you were the star of this show. You wouldn't give me any shit."

"Ohhh," I said excitedly, "I sure wouldn't!"

"Maybe I should take you under my wing or something."

"I like being taken… under things," I stammered.

He admired his chiseled face in the scratched bathroom mirror. "Course, I couldn't do it while you have that drag queen attached to your hip."

"Drag queen?"

"Kurt. He's really funny, but he's so over-the-top."

I knew Phillip was right. Kurt was fearless, but that lack of fear also meant that he didn't know when to quit. A combo plate of Rosalind Russell and Liberace—all big hair and snappy one-liners—he was about as subtle as an elevator whose cable has snapped.

"I guess I feel sorry for him," I stammered, trying to figure out a proper response. "He needs a friend, you know?"

"Well, it doesn't have to be you."

• • •

I began ignoring Kurt. The more I thought about it, the more it seemed like the right thing to do. Since Phillip thought Kurt was embarrassing, and since Tommy Tune—a heterosexual actor/dancer/director/choreographer—would not want to be involved with someone like that, either, it was incumbent upon me to shun Kurt and teach him the moral and spiritual error of his ways.

Then, Phillip—because I was no longer hanging out with Kurt—began spending more time with me at the bar. My star was clearly on the ascent, and I realized that, as long as I kept our relationship on a strictly professional level, all would be right with God and Tommy Tune.

Everything seemed to be going swimmingly, other than the occasional confrontation with Kurt, who—in typically overbearing fashion—demanded to know why I was ignoring him.

"You're imagining things," I said as I edged away.

"What's the *real* reason?" he whispered, jerking his head in Phillip's direction. "Bigger name?"

"I cannot help it," I huffed, "that Phillip sees something in me."

"I'll *bet* he does."

"What's that supposed to mean?"

"I'm beginning to think you're the only one," Kurt replied, "who *doesn't* see it in you."

• • •

Several nights later, as Dad and I performed our ritual sterilization of the house in preparation for Mother's return from work, the phone rang.

"It's for you!" Dad called out.

I tiptoed into the family room. "If it's Kurt…" I whispered.

"It's somebody named Phillip."

"I'll take it in my room!"

I stumbled to my bedroom and slammed the door, taking several deep breaths before picking up the phone. "Well, well, well, Mr. Conway," I said. "Am I in trouble?"

"Yeah," he replied. "You're gonna need to be spanked." I almost dropped the phone. "My place, tonight. Ten o'clock." He was gone.

My heart was beating so loudly that I did not even realize that I could hear the television in our family room… through the telephone.

• • •

"We're having a sleepover at the choreographer's house so we can work on our dance routines," I lied to Mother and Dad.

"Who's 'we'?" Dad asked.

"The chorus."

"The whole chorus?" Mother asked. "Boys *and* girls?"

"Oh, no," I interrupted, suddenly realizing the implication of possible assignations. "Just the guys."

"Why," Dad chimed in, shaking a bit, "do you have to stay overnight?"

"Oh, it's just likely to run really late."

"Well, you know, I really could, uh…" Dad paused, groping for words.

"Spit it out, Ray," Mother snapped. "I've got paneling to polish."

"I need some help repainting the patio."

"At night?" I replied. "I don't think the bug zapper provides enough light."

"Your mother really wants it done."

"Oh, it can wait until tomorrow," Mother said airily to Dad. "Long as it's done by noon."

"Thanks!" I replied, racing down the hall before they could change their minds.

"But if we find out there were girls there…" Mother yelled after me.

"Oh, don't worry!" I hollered back.

I barely noticed the strange whimpering sound emanating from my father.

• • •

It was 9:30 p.m. as I piloted my Chevy Malibu through the streets of the Central West End. Growing more and more nervous, I pulled over and parked, far from a streetlight so that no one could see into the car.

"We're just friends," I said aloud to my reflection in the rearview mirror as I checked my highly damaged hairdo under the dome light. "But God," I said softly, pleadingly, "just for grins, let's say this *was*, like, a 'gay' thing. Maybe I should just get it out of my system once and for all."

I envisioned Phillip and me in bed together, about to consummate the act. Having no real idea what to expect, my mind's camera panned over to the window for a lingering shot of the moonlight as, from high above, God blessed this one-time man-on-man action with a giant, heavenly thumbs-up. The next morning, I would awaken to find Phillip standing over the bed with a silver tray, on which was a Denny's Grand Slam breakfast and a glass of Tang, and I imagined thanking him for helping me push courageously through this brief gay phase to emerge a confident heterosexual.

It was 10:05. I pulled into the driveway of Gary's home, having circled the block for ten minutes so as not to seem desperate. The looming three-story house was quiet, dark, and somehow ominous, like the Disneyland haunted mansion without the souvenir shop. After a series of short, hyperventi-lated breaths, I rang the bell, and Phillip appeared at the door wearing a shortie robe.

"Did I wake you up?" I said stupidly, as scenes from *The Graduate*, which I had just seen at a classic film festival at school, flashed through my mind. Phillip was about to be just like Mrs. Robinson.

But younger. And a dude.

"Yeah," he laughed. "Let's get to bed."

He pulled me in the door and, without a word, led me by the hand up that grand, creaky staircase to the second floor.

"Boy, I love this house," I chattered nervously as we passed various rooms. "How tall are these ceilings, like a thousand feet?" I stuck my head into an unused bedroom, trying to slow Phillip down. "Man, it seems like every room has a fireplace.

Can you imagine having to clean all these out? Whew!" I began to sing. "Chim chiminey, chim chiminey, chim chim cheree…"

Phillip lifted his finger to his lips to shush me. "I'm not allowed to bring tricks here," he whispered.

"Do you wanna rehearse?" I whispered as he headed toward the last room at the end of the hall.

"No," he replied, chuckling. "I think I've got it down." It occurred to me that perhaps we were not talking about the same thing.

He led me into the bedroom, which was dark, save for a roaring fire in the fireplace. It was probably sixty-eight degrees in the house, but sweat was now streaming out of every available pore on my body as though I had prop hoses in a wig on my head. He closed the door.

"Are you warm?" I chattered, fanning myself. "It's really toasty in here. Or is it just me? I tend to run a little hot. So does my mother. She keeps their bedroom window open in the winter. Sometimes it freezes open and Dad has to blow-torch it to get it closed. She's like, 'It's not cold in here,' and Dad's like, 'There's *frost on the mirror.*'"

Phillip leaned in, his lips touching my bad ear. I think he said, "This should cool you off," or possibly, "This is just like golf." It didn't matter. I felt a chill run down my spine as he began to demonstrate exactly how nonprocreational sex was done.

An hour later, as I lay on the bed, awed by the variety of festivities possible, I realized that it might take two or three episodes to fully vanquish this whole gay thing. Thank God it was only 11:00 p.m.

"Ready for round two?" I said in a voice that I imagined to be very Captain Stubing, but was probably more Vicki Stubing.

He sat up and retrieved his robe. "It's getting late. I gotta get up early."

He moved to the edge of the bed and slipped his arms into his robe.

What was happening? Panic began to rise inside me. My opportunity to solidify my straightness, to make God and Tommy proud, was evaporating before my eyes. I had to get this train back on the tracks, and fast.

I tried to slip the robe back over his shoulders, but he yanked it on and stood up.

"I should let you go."

• • •

As I made the forty-minute drive home, I anguished over Phillip's sudden indifference. Surely, he was just tired—it must be the rehearsals catching up with him. I hadn't been inadequate, had I?

I imagined doing this with someone else, and Phillip finding out, then going insane with jealousy as he tried to fight the other guy in a Sharks-versus-Jets showdown.

Consumed as I was by the idea of us singing "Tonight" from *West Side Story* on the rooftop of the parking garage at school, the sun setting over the A&W's "Two-fer Tuesdays" sign, I completely forgot that I was not supposed to have returned home until morning.

Mother—who was, according to Dad, undergoing "the change, God help us all"—met me at the door in her bikini, a tattered two-piece that was safety-pinned together, holding a stack of freshly pressed bath towels, followed by Dad, a strangely hopeful look on his face.

"What are you doing back?"

"Oh. Right," I stammered as I groped for an excuse. "Yeah, I wasn't supposed to be, huh?"

Think. Think fast.

"There were girls there."

"Ohhhh." Mother smiled. "Well, that's great. We're very proud of you." She elbowed Dad. "I guess all those Bible tapes have finally paid off."

• • •

A week passed. Two after-parties. No Phillip.

We had not spoken since our night together, and I was beginning to panic.

That asshole Kurt, on the other hand, was loving every minute. He would elbow the other chorus members with glee as Phillip gave us instructions without ever once singling me out for a wink. He would stand with a gaggle of girls at the bar, drinking in Phillip's disinterest as I attempted to cheer Phillip on at pool. He savored every indifferent moment with the overwrought glee and elation of an amphetamine-fueled party clown.

A week before opening night, the cast met at the local Shakey's for the all-you-can-eat pizza buffet, a $3.99 cornucopia of dried-out carbohydrates. I was nearly unable to enjoy my eleven slices of pizza, what with Kurt basking in the glow of Phillip's once again unexplained absence.

Finally, I could stand it no longer. Calling silently upon my dramatic gifts, I nonchalantly turned to Gary.

"Where's Phillip?" I said with studied disinterest.

"Oh," Gary replied, munching on a piece of thin-crust sausage, "he's on a date. With a guy from Oak Tree."

Members of the cast murmured appreciatively. It was widely known that the Oak Tree menswear stores only hired superhot salespeople.

The news hit me like a freight train. "What can I say?" Gary added, apparently unaware of the force of his blow. "He likes the pretty ones."

I smiled, even as I felt tears begin to well up in my eyes. Tears that had no justification, no logic. Why on earth should I be upset at him dating someone—even if it *was* against the laws of God and nature? He was on the highway to hell, not me.

Determined not to show my disappointment, I stole a glance at Kurt, who I was certain would be wetting his pants at this latest development, but he just looked down at his plate, picking at a six-inch pile of mojo potatoes and cheesy cheese bread.

● ● ●

At the next rehearsal, I just stared at Phillip silently, my angry eyes boring holes into his guilty, shameful skull. What had I done to deserve this?

After an hour of humiliation, I slipped out the side door and sat down against the wall of the brick building, alone. How would I get through this last week of rehearsal and the shows? And how could he not realize what he was doing to me?

Suddenly, the door flew open. Phillip sauntered out, lighting a cigarette. I turned away and steeled myself as I heard him inhale deeply. A thick cloud of smoke whooshed into my sightline, hanging suspended in the cool night air. I continued to gaze out at the parking lot, attempting to be fascinated by one of my professors, who was making out with a pretty blonde student in his Delta 88.

Silence. Another toke. The smoke sailed into view again.

"Could you quit blowing that in my face?"

"Sorry. Jeez." Another toke. "Is something wrong?"

"You could have at least told me!"

"What?" he replied, a bit taken aback at my fury. "Told you *what?*"

"About Oak Tree guy."

He snorted. "What is there to tell?"

"You went out on a date with him."

"Yeah, so?"

"Well, I just think it would have been the considerate thing to do."

"Oh, gee, I'm sorry," he replied. "I didn't realize my personal life was any of your business."

"We were boyfriends!" I exploded, horrified at the words almost before I'd finished them. I wanted to snatch them from the air and stuff them back into my mouth. "Well, I mean…"

"Boyfriends?" he laughed. "We tricked. How does that make us boyfriends?"

"Well, I didn't mean like *real* boyfriends…" I tried to cover my tracks, but it was far too late. "I just meant…"

"Look, Eric," he said, chuckling as he took another hit off the Marlboro. "You're a nice kid and all…" He flipped his cigarette onto the pavement, the glowing ember rolling across the cement. I wanted to pick it up and throw it at him. "But…" The side door flew open again. "I don't do repeats."

Kurt stepped outside. He glanced at the two of us, aware that something was going on. Had he heard Phillip? My mortification ratcheted up another notch.

Without a word, Kurt turned and walked back inside, pulling the door closed behind him. Phillip paused for a moment, as though he was going to say something else, then grabbed the handle and yanked the door open. "Break's over!" he yelled to the crowd gathered in the lobby.

Five more minutes passed as I tried in vain to work up the courage to return to rehearsal.

I wanted to quit. I wanted to run. Maybe I could transfer to Yale. Or Juilliard. Or Miss Hickey's Secretarial School. I had heard rumors that there would be bumps on the path to artistic fulfillment, but I didn't realize there would also be sinkholes.

Finally, I took a deep breath and pulled myself to my feet. I turned to head to the door just as it opened. It was Kurt.

"Aren't you supposed to be inside?" I sniped.

"Yeah," he replied quietly. "I just came to see if you were okay."

• • •

Kurt took me back.

We talked for hours that night, as he accepted my contrition with dignity and grace, thoughtfully pretending to care about my time with Phillip.

"Tell me about that night," he said excitedly, "and don't leave anything out."

Then I, in turn, accepted him, graciously and almost without reservation, when he delivered some news of his own.

"Would we still be friends if I told you that…" He hesitated. "I think *I* might be gay."

"Well," I replied courageously, patting his hand, "the Bible says to hate the sin and love the sinner."

Kurt rolled his eyes.

"So… yes," I added. "I will still be your friend."

In the ensuing days, as Phillip now completely ignored me, I realized that God had given me a sign: it was time to put the homo behind me. The evil that had held me in its exotic grasp had been purged from my soul. I could now focus on my theatrical career, and on saving Kurt. For I had learned that God truly did want us to love one another—there were just, in the case of people like Phillip, parameters to that love. Loving Kurt for who he was (regardless of the leaky-rowboat-on-the-lake-of-fire implications for Kurt) was good; loving Phillip in a weird, physical kind of way wasn't.

And I imagined Tommy Tune, his eyes sparkling with pride, giving me a big, fat heterosexual high kick.

Chapter 6

IF THEY COULD
SEE ME NOW

The Pajama Game was a smash hit, running all three scheduled performances to nearly sold-out houses, thanks to a large cast and the compulsory attendance of family and friends. And as I took my bows with the other members of the chorus, I found myself bowled over by the feeling of warmth and acceptance from these audiences who seemed eager to show their appreciation and wrap up the evening in time to get home for Johnny Carson.

This acknowledgment of my talent was the same feeling I had gotten from my trumpet solos and was a welcome distraction from the humiliation I had suffered at Phillip's hands. While God clearly didn't approve of my experimentation with homosexuality, he did approve of my desire to wear tap shoes and makeup.

So I began my search for another show, one that would allow me to spread my artistic wings and soar, to become the

Tommy Tune of a new generation. This next time, I thought, I will have a character with a *name*.

The theatrical productions of Debra Kingston, my voice and dance teacher, were nearly-award-nominated events of the sort rarely seen at two-year colleges in northeast St. Louis County. Her latest directorial effort was to be the exciting, Tony award–overlooked *You're a Good Man, Charlie Brown*.

Since there was no other musical at the University of Missouri that season, I decided to audition. And, to my utter shock and elation, I was cast.

My shock did not come from the fact that I had been awarded a role, of course, for it seemed as though I were being led to a life in the theater. What was both thrilling and life changing was that in this, only my second musical, I was awarded the lead.

Being chosen to star as the iconic Charlie Brown was electrifying. Overnight, I realized, I had gone from the chorus to the starring role—just like Shirley MacLaine in the Broadway run of *The Pajama Game*. The parallels were not lost on me, and I began to wonder if perhaps this was a portent, a sign from above that Shirley was actually the star whose life and career I was destined to replicate.

I went to visit Kurt, who had just gotten a job hawking hosiery at the Famous-Barr department store and was unable to audition for the show.

"If… they… could… see me now, that little gang of mine," I sang softly, high-stepping across the sock department, doffing an invisible top hat as I reprised MacLaine's song from the musical *Sweet Charity*.

"Why are you singing a song about a hooker?" Kurt said. He gasped. "Did you get a role in the show?"

"I have," I replied excitedly, "been plucked from obscurity to *star* as Charlie Brown!"

"But you're like nine feet tall," he replied. "You'll be the world's largest cartoon character."

"Don't you get it?" I said, my head filled with visions of champagne and opening night telegrams. "My career path. It's just like Shirley MacLaine."

MacLaine was a sweet, bubbly girl who, barely out of high school, had been pulled from the chorus of *Pajama Game* to go on for the star, Carol Haney, when Carol hurt her ankle. Hal B. Wallis, a famous producer, was in the audience that night, and he signed Shirley to a five-year movie contract, which made her a movie star. She then went on to star in television specials and write a memoir. The theater had been her launching pad for a career that spanned nearly every possible artistic discipline.

"Does this mean," Kurt replied as he restocked the size-large nude panty hose, "that you're gonna start wearing a pageboy hairdo and sequined pantsuits?"

I ignored him, my head spinning. I was already an actor/singer/dancer, so I was ostensibly prepared for Broadway, TV, and movies. And since I had spent most of my high school years passing notes to my female friends in class—featuring a wide and impressive variety of anatomical insults—perhaps I could eventually add author to my credits. Maybe I could be a quadruple threat, too.

Who, I wondered excitedly, would launch my career? Who might be in the audience when I went on as Charlie Brown?

• • •

As I read the entire play that night at home, I realized how fortunate it was that Kurt hadn't auditioned, since the kind of brassy, over-the-top role he was suited for did not exist in male form in this show.

It did, however, exist in female form, and Mandy, a pretty, eighteen-year-old blonde with a spectacular voice was cast as Lucy. I was immediately as drawn to her as I was to Kurt—perhaps because she was, for all intents and purposes, a soprano version of him, albeit with an off switch.

Jason, a teen-idol type with annoyingly big blue eyes, was awarded the role of the blanket-obsessed Linus. As the show's namesake star, I might normally have subscribed to the ugly bridesmaids theory in surrounding myself with a supporting cast. But a handsome actor like Jason, I reasoned, might raise my game, so I graciously embraced his casting.

Somewhat lesser talents, I felt, were cast in the secondary roles of Snoopy, Schroeder, and Patty, a character so ill defined in the comic strip that none of us were even sure who she was, other than that she wasn't *Peppermint* Patty—a considerable relief to my friend Candace, who was awarded the role and, as a good Christian, did not relish the idea of dressing like a blossoming lesbian.

Candace did not begin dating any of the other male members of the cast, most likely because she was saving herself for the Oak Ridge Boys, a groupie pipe dream I didn't have the heart to dispel. But Mandy and I quickly became an item, a situation that was clearly more her idea than mine.

"Oh, the leads always get together," Mandy said

matter-of-factly as she grabbed my arm and draped it around her waist. She had been performing since she was barely a teen and was a consummate professional, knowledgeable in all things theatrical, and she wasn't hesitant to take charge. "The creation of art is an intense experience," she explained, "and since we're sharing it, it's only natural that we make out."

I was, I had to admit, caught a bit off guard. Since the Phillip incident, I had decided that relationships were a distraction from the larger pursuit of stardom, and that my best course of action when it came to the opposite sex would be inaction.

But Mandy was having none of that.

"Everyone!" she hollered, clapping her hands to quiet the other cast members. "Eric and I are, as you might expect, a thing. Now, we hope you'll honor the fact that our intimate personal relationship is not for public consumption. While it's natural for the stars to take solace in one another's arms, ours is a much deeper and more profound commitment. So, please, let's keep the gossip to a minimum."

"And we resolve to do the same," I added, trying to appear nonchalant about this sudden and unauthorized elevation of our relationship, "should any of you decide to get busy."

This, of course, seemed somewhat unlikely, given that Candace was the only other female, and, although quite comely, with feathered blond hair, porcelain skin, and delicate bone structure, she exuded the raw sexuality of a Vacation Bible School teacher.

Although a dating relationship with Mandy had not been anywhere on my to-do list, I found myself rather enthusiastically embracing the attention that came with my starring role as both Charlie Brown *and* Mandy's boyfriend. Debra, the other cast members, even other students at the school seemed to view me as both an artist and a stud—labels that had rarely been conferred upon me, and certainly never simultaneously.

Celebrity status, I had to admit, was intoxicating. Mandy and I would sweep into the theater lobby, arm in arm, basking in the delicious looks of admiration and resentment from those who were, sadly, both unattached and unknown. It seemed as if the world truly was becoming my oyster.

Of course, dating Mandy required a certain amount of physical interaction, if only for the keeping up of appearances, and Mandy wasn't shy about mentioning it.

"Can I ask you something?" Mandy said one evening as I drove her home after rehearsal.

"Sure," I said, glancing at myself in the rearview mirror to admire the glow that seemed to permeate my being now. That inner glow of celebrity.

"How come you never wanna make out?"

"What are you talking about?" I said defensively. "We made out last night."

"You kissed me goodbye. On the cheek."

"I have to focus," I said firmly. "We are the show's stars. This musical rides on our shoulders."

"It's an *ensemble* show," she replied.

"People are coming to see Charlie Brown and Lucy," I replied. "Nobody gives a shit about Patty or Schroeder. If the show fails," I said with gravity, "*we* have failed."

• • •

In support of my newfound notoriety, I made an excursion

to the local screen printer at the mall—with Candace in tow—where we had raglan-sleeve T-shirts made for the cast with *You're a Good Man, Charlie Brown* ironed on in glittery rainbow-colored bubble letters. We also added to the back, at considerable extra cost, the words *Official Cast*, to confirm our club's exclusivity and dissuade any lesser community college actors from attempting to cash in on our fame.

For the first time since my days as a trumpet soloist, I felt admired, envied, almost despised by those around me. It was a heady feeling, this sense that others were merely tiny, insignificant planets orbiting around a large, gaseous star.

"Eric, can I see you for a moment?"

It was a Tuesday afternoon, and we were in the middle of rehearsal.

"Take five, everybody," Debra said as I crossed down to where she was sitting in the theater. She turned to me. "Let's go for a little walk."

She led me outside, and we began to stroll among the leafy grounds of the commons. Debra was a very pretty blonde, petite and thirtyish, and she linked her arm in mine as we walked.

"I've been wanting to talk to you about something," she said quietly. "I'm a little bit concerned about your performance."

I turned to look at her, shocked. What could I possibly be doing wrong, I wondered? Sure, essaying the role of an underdog who spends his life trying to fight his way out of his own insecurities was a bit of a stretch for me, but Debra had clearly felt that I had the chops to pull this off.

"It seems as if you're more concerned about singing the

songs well than creating a character."

"Well," I replied defensively, "it *is* a musical."

"Of course it is. But it doesn't matter how well the back row can hear your vibrato if you don't create a compelling character."

"I'm just trying to amp him up a little. He's kinda boring."

"Charlie Brown's this sweet little boy who's an underdog," she said patiently. "He's not boring, he's insecure." She glanced up at me. "I'm guessing at some point in your life you must have felt that way, right? Everyone does."

"Yeah, sure," I said hesitantly. "I suppose."

"You want to make the audience root for him," she replied. "Finding that vulnerability will completely change the dynamic of your performance. Do you understand what I mean?"

"Of course," I lied.

"What did Debra want?" Mandy whispered a few minutes later as we took our places for the next scene.

"Ummm…" I replied, loath to admit the truth, "she just wanted to tell me how glad she was to have discovered me."

"Oh, really?" Mandy said thoughtfully. "*Huh.*"

• • •

It had never quite occurred to me that essaying a role like Charlie Brown would be difficult. I had been so caught up in the notion of stardom that I guess I had assumed that a star-*making* performance meant just singing balls out. Did I really know how to act?

Playing a member of the chorus in *The Pajama Game*, my face mostly hidden by scenery and performers with lines, had seemed so easy. But standing downstage center, alone, singing a song about loneliness, was, apparently, not so easy.

Is this, I wondered, *how Shirley MacLaine felt when she first stepped into the spotlight?*

I summoned Kurt to the self-service gas station where I now worked.

"So," he said, taking a seat on the floor of the kiosk so as not to be spotted by my boss, who had an annoying penchant for drive-bys, "how goes rehearsal?"

"Okay," I replied hesitantly. "Debra says I'm singing the hell out of the songs."

"Hmmm," he replied as he slurped his omnipresent Coke. "That's an interesting comment. I don't think of those songs as showstoppers."

"Well," I sniffed, "she apparently doesn't, either. She told me to reel it in a little."

"Why? What did you do?"

"Nothing!"

"Are you playing it like you're Evita standing on the balcony of the Casa Rosada?"

I sighed. "I'm just trying to make Charlie Brown interesting. I don't know why no one understands that."

"I know," he said in a tone that implied commiseration. "You're just trying to be something you're not."

"What's that supposed to mean?" I snapped.

He shook the ice in his cup. "Well, I mean, come on, you're dating Mandy."

"So?" I replied. "It happens all the time with the stars of a show. You know, the intensity of the creative process and—"

"Seems to me you might be a big homo."

"Oh, please. I had one little experimentation. That's what people do in college."

"Girls experiment. Guys draw *conclusions*. I think you're dating her," he said, sucking the final drops of Coke from his cup, "because you're always concerned about appearances."

"That's ridiculous," I retorted, glancing at my reflection in the bulletproof glass. I really needed to get some sun.

"So maybe the same thing's happening with your acting. Maybe you're more worried about being seen as a 'star' than in being real."

"Stars," I said, "give bravura performances. Stars knock people's socks off."

"But the reason people love Shirley MacLaine in *Sweet Charity*," Kurt said, snatching a pack of Red Vines from the candy display, "is because they can see Charity's self-doubt." He tore into them like a wolf over a bloody carcass as he scanned the candy display. "You got any Mallomars?"

• • •

What did Shirley have that I didn't have, I wondered as I drove Mandy and I home from rehearsal the next night. How would Hal Wallis see my potential and sign me to a five-year contract if I wasn't displaying my full range of talent? Did I *have* a full range of talent?

And was Hal Wallis still alive?

As I silently pondered the very real possibility of failure, Mandy performed her nightly nonstop monologue, filling the air with her opinions on a wide variety of topics.

"When TV stardom is attainable simply by having double-D boobs," she declared, "it's time to throw your TV off a cliff."

"I'm sorry," she announced, "but the fact that *Smokey and the Bandit 1* was a piece of dog shit should not be encouragement to make *Smokey and the Bandit 2*."

"Here's why Barbra Streisand shouldn't sing disco."

As I pulled my silver Chevy Malibu into her driveway, Hamletta turned to me suddenly. "You've been kinda quiet."

I took a deep breath. "Umm," I said nervously as I put the car in park, "there's something I need to talk to you about."

"Oh, God," she replied, dread in her voice. "Well, I guess I knew this was coming." She sighed. "I've gotta stop dating guys in the theater."

"Debra thinks," I said quietly, "that I'm not really connected to my character."

"Wait... what?"

"She thinks I'm playing Charlie Brown too 'big.'"

"Well, sure you are," Mandy replied, an odd tone of relief in her voice. "Everybody knows that."

"Why?!"

"You're up there acting like Chita Rivera on her third encore."

"Rude!"

"Look," she said softening, "you're just afraid to show your vulnerability. Lots of actors who are sort of, you know, new to the craft are."

"I am very in touch with my feelings!" I hollered.

"Yeah, I'm not so sure about that." She turned to face me. "Let me ask you something. What were you like as a kid?"

"Listen," I said, irritated. "I've taken *several* theater classes. I know all about that sense memory crap."

"Just humor me. What was your childhood like?"

"Like everybody else's," I snapped. "It was fine."

"So, it was all Richie Cunningham, sunshine and rainbows?"

"Enough, I guess…" I really wasn't interested in this method-acting bullshit.

"So, not entirely."

"I suppose I wasn't superpopular," I said. "But, you know, I had my outlets, so it was all fine."

"What kind of outlets?"

"Just, you know, imaginary stuff."

"Oh," she cooed, "I love that kind of thing. Tell me."

"I don't know…" I said, stalling.

I had never told another human being about my childhood pastime, and I wasn't at all sure that I wanted to start now, even with this beautiful, bossy, talented girl that I did, in fact, trust.

"Well," I said hesitantly, "I used to, kind of, pretend I was Endora from *Bewitched*."

"What?"

"It made me feel better."

"Endora? You pretended you were Endora?"

"See, this is exactly why—"

"I'm sorry," she said, chuckling. "It's just not the kind of thing you hear every day."

I started the car.

"Wait," she said. "It's nothing to be embarrassed about."

"Great."

"So, why Endora?"

"She was powerful. She took no prisoners."

"Hmmm," she replied thoughtfully. "So you were trying to do magic?"

"Yeah."

"Why?"

"It just sorta helped me escape," I said quietly.

Mandy put her hand on top of mine. "Escape what?"

This conversation was uncomfortable—even more uncomfortable than I had thought it would be, and I was not particularly jazzed about reliving all these memories. Mandy gazed at me questioningly.

"Bullies," I said, finally. "A mother who made me rake myself into my bedroom every night with a shag-carpet rake. People dying. The usual stuff."

"People dying?"

I gazed out at the parking lot, dotted with Ford Pintos that hadn't blown up yet. "My great-grandma. Our best friends' mom."

"What happened to your friends' mom?"

"Cancer. She was gutted like a fish." I felt a lump forming in my throat. "It was… bad."

Mandy was quiet for a moment. She looked up at me. "How did you feel right before you performed your magic?"

How did I *feel*? I'd never really thought about it. And I didn't really want to think about it now. I swallowed hard, trying to push the lump down.

"I don't know. Scared, I guess. I just wanted to make the bad feelings go away."

"Did you? By being Endora?"

"Sometimes."

Mandy smiled at me with a look of gentle understanding. "That feeling, right before you did your magic," she said quietly, "is the essence of Charlie Brown."

• • •

It was opening night, and I sat in the dressing room getting ready to go on.

I hadn't had the courage to put Mandy's words into practice. As much as I knew she was probably right—and as much as doing so might have given me the star-making performance I craved—there was a reason I had never set foot into my grade school, my junior high, or my high school since leaving them. I wanted to put the often-ugly past behind me.

"Jesus," Jason, the actor playing Linus, said as he glanced over and noticed the makeup I had applied. "Are you playing Charlie Brown or Lucy?"

There was a knock at the door.

"Is everybody decent?"

"Hey," I said, waving Mandy in. She looked adorable in her Lucy dress.

"I just wanted to tell you guys to break a leg," she said brightly. "Are you nervous?"

"Nope," Jason replied.

"Yep," I replied.

"Don't be," she said to me. "Just remember..." She leaned over and whispered into my good ear, "Endora wants you to be great."

She skipped out.

"Who's Endora?" Jason said as he laced up his tennis shoes and winked at me. "Is that your drag name?"

• • •

I stood in the wings, watching Jason, as Linus, singing "My Blanket and Me." You just wanted to hug him. As Linus, of course.

We were partway through act one, and I was about to sing a solo about flying a kite—a song that, in all its simplicity, summed up Charlie Brown's feelings of inadequacy.

I desperately wished I could make Debra proud. I desperately wished I could give a performance that would earn me the overnight success of Shirley MacLaine. But I just couldn't. It wasn't worth dredging up the kind of memories I had taken pains to push aside.

I had muddled through the opening number, "You're a Good Man, Charlie Brown," where the other characters gave their insulting opinions of Charlie Brown. And I did, I thought, a commendable job of seeming put-upon. But I had no other characters to play off for this next song. It was just me and an invisible kite.

As I watched Jason charm the audience with his sweet panic at the thought of losing his precious blanket, I suddenly flashed upon a moment, some eight years earlier, when I had been last picked for a sixth-grade softball game. I had always dreaded the at-bat moment and had, in fact, found ways to escape it as often as possible. But there was no escaping it on this sunny spring day, and I crept into the batter's box with the dread of a death-row inmate. It would be humiliating. My classmates would, as they always did, laugh about it for weeks to come.

The strains of music onstage, the lights, and the chaos backstage all disappeared as that softball field began to surround my vision, and, in my imagination, I picked up the heavy wooden bat.

"Hurry up, let's get it over with," my bully, John, yelled to the pitcher. I was gonna strike out. I always did.

Back inside the Florissant Valley Community College theater, the stage manager whispered, "Go!"

And as I made my entrance to the opening notes of the song, holding my kite, in my mind, I held a bat.

"Little more speed, little more rope," I sang, "little more wind, little more hope. Gotta get this stupid kite to fly..."

On the softball field of Brown Elementary, I lifted the bat to my shoulder and assumed the stance. In an effort to embarrass me further, Mike, the pitcher, lobbed an embarrassingly easy ball my way. I swung.

"Strike one!"

Titters floated across from the bench. Even my own teammates, who had something to lose, couldn't help but laugh.

"Little less speed, little more tack, little less rise, little more slack, gotta keep my wits about me now..."

Mike wound up and lobbed another wussy ball my way. I swung again.

"Strike two!"

"Millions of kids do it every day, they make a kite and poof, it's in the sky... Leave it to me to have the one fool kite that likes to see a little kid cry."

It was the strangest thing. The energy of the audience seemed to be shifting. I noticed people in the first two rows—which were all I could see—leaning forward, almost as if willing me to get that kite in the air.

"Little less talk, little more skill, little less luck, little more will, gotta face this fellow eye to eye..."

Mike, who now clearly just wanted to get me out of the batter's box and get on with the game, wound up for strike number three and, this time, lobbed a fastball my way. I swung again.

CRACK.

I had no idea what had just happened.

"Run!" John yelled.

"Wait a minute—what's it doing? It isn't on the ground. It's in the air!"

I looked up to see one of the outfielders running back, back, back, looking skyward. I had not only connected my bat with the ball, I had sent it careening to the far reaches of the outfield.

I took off for first base.

"Look at that—it's caught the breeze now..."

"Keep going!" I heard someone yell. I rounded second base.

"It's past the trees now..."

Third base. "Go for home!"

"With room to spare..."

Even with one bad ear, I suddenly realized that my teammates were cheering. I had hit a home run.

As I approached home plate, I met a barrage of raised hands, all awaiting high fives. I slowed down and slapped every palm with the most wondrous feeling of pride and accomplishment that I had ever felt. I was, in that one brief and shining moment, one of the boys.

"Oh, what a beautiful sight! And I'm not such a clumsy guy. If I really try, I can really fly a..."

"I suppose," my bully John said loudly from the end of the line of cheering teammates, the only one not holding his hand up, "even fairies get lucky once in a while."

And on the stage of the Florissant Valley Community College theater, my kite made a sudden beeline for the ground and crashed. I looked down at it, first stunned, then unsurprised, and sighed wistfully. Somehow, even my moments of triumph were followed by a swift kick in the nuts.

And then, from the audience, I heard a couple little whimpers of empathy, the sort of involuntary reactions that expose a kindred recognition.

$$\bullet \quad \bullet \quad \bullet$$

"You got a standing ovation!"

Jason and Candace and the others crowded around Mandy and me, high-fiving. "Way to go!"

The crew surrounded the six of us backstage, everyone gleefully celebrating a show that had gone off pretty much without a hitch. And as I stood in the middle of the circle, somewhat shocked at my own last-minute choice to relive the pain of my youth, and stunned at how the audience had embraced it, I realized that, indeed, anything was possible.

Maybe I *could* be Shirley MacLaine. Maybe a future in Broadway shows, movies, and publishing *was* on tap.

Everyone was hugging and kissing. I leaned over and planted one squarely on Mandy's mouth. She lit up.

I leaned over and planted one squarely on Jason's mouth. He didn't light up so much.

I rushed out to the lobby to meet my parents.

"Congratulations!" Mother said, hugging me in an uncommon and impromptu display of physical affection, which was thrilling. "You were wonderful!"

I held on to her for a brief moment, savoring this closeness we had so rarely shared. Her pride was palpable, and I wanted to bask in the glow.

"Yeah," Dad chimed in. "But what's with all the makeup? You looked more like Charlene Brown."

Note taken, I thought. Tomorrow night, maybe I'd pull back a little on the rouge.

"Could you tell," I said excitedly, "if there were any producers in the audience?"

···· Chapter 7 ····

DON'T CALL ME SHIRLEY

To my disappointment, I was not catapulted directly onto
the stages of the Great White Way. As gratifying as it was
to feel that I had conquered my fear of being vulnerable
onstage, Actors Equity wasn't exactly begging me to join.
The Westport Playhouse and the Missouri Rep—high-class,
professional theaters whose actors made dozens of dollars per
show—had not called.

I knew that America's biggest musical theater superstars
were triple threats—actors, dancers, *and* singers. And I certainly longed to be threatening in multiple ways. So I began to
take stock of my talents.

My acting ability seemed to be gaining a bit of steam on its
own, so I felt fairly confident in that department. But when it
came to hoofing, I knew intrinsically that I would never premiere a ballet with Baryshnikov, since coordination and I were
infrequently on speaking terms.

However, I did possess a strong baritone voice. This, I decided, would become my area of expertise, my secret weapon—the talent that would have lesser triples gnashing their teeth as they downgraded themselves to doubles.

But where to begin? The voice lessons provided by Debra Kingston had served me well in this early stage of my career. But Debra was merely a professor who gave lessons on the side. Perhaps it was time, I thought, for a real professional instructor—someone who could take my instrument to the next level.

Although the cast of *Charlie Brown* had mostly lost touch after we ended our run (Mandy breaking up with me because she felt I had "other avenues to pursue"), I remained close with Candace. And together, she and I began our search for a coach who had taught the greatest voices of our time—people like Barbra Streisand, Hall & Oates, and Tennille (but not the Captain, who, from the looks of things, was mute).

"I want someone," I said, as we sat at the A&W near school, scarfing down fifty-cent chili dogs and leafing through the St. Louis yellow pages, "who can take me to New York *and beyond.*"

"Beyond what?" Candace asked.

I sighed. Candace had no designs on a career on the stage. New York was, as far as she was concerned, the first city God planned to wipe off the map during Armageddon.

"I'm not taking voice lessons to become a star," she said. "I just wanna do a little performing and improve myself."

"Well, what on earth," I replied indignantly, "is the point of *that?*"

Candace looked at me intently. "Why do you wanna be a star so bad?"

"Because it'll make my parents proud of me," I answered without even thinking.

She paused. "Is there a reason they wouldn't be proud of you?"

I called Kurt.

"I've decided to take voice lessons," I told him as he crunched potato chips in my ear. "I figure I should get as much training as possible before I leave for New York."

"New York? You're moving to New York to become a chorine?"

I rolled my eyes. When it came to gayness, Kurt had really committed, far more than was either necessary or within reason.

"I'm *hoping*," I said patiently, "to transfer to Juilliard or NYU. And then, you know, while starring as the Scarecrow in an all-white student production of *The Wiz*, or something, I'll be asked to costar in a TV special with Shirley MacLaine."

"You do realize that Shirley MacLaine can dance."

"Yeah, so?"

"And you fell off the stage during *Pajama Game* rehearsals."

"I've gotten better!"

Shirley MacLaine was a hoofer who used acting and singing to support her brilliance with the dance. I was, I hoped, simply an inverse image: a brilliant singer who used my acting and dancing as methods of exhibiting my vocal finesse.

• • •

Candace and I finally found a vocal coach with an impressive résumé—he had guided the careers of no fewer than three community theater stars, one of whom had gone on to fame and fortune as a local weatherman. Leonard was a somewhat short, mercurial man with dark-brown hair and a penchant for Hawaiian shirts that camouflaged his potbelly. I judged him to be about forty, which meant that he surely had an enormous amount of show business wisdom due to the sheer number of decades he had spent on the planet.

His studio was in an office building in Kirkwood, an upscale suburb of ivy-covered homes. Any vocal coach who could afford such glamorous digs must be worth his weight in gold, I thought. And indeed, we were required to audition to see if our talents merited an investment of his time and energy.

"Let's start with some simple scales," he said as he sat behind the baby grand piano, sizing me up like a butcher inspecting a side of grade-C beef.

I dutifully obliged.

He seemed impressed. I increased my volume to display the breadth and power of my resonant vibrato, trying to fill the room with magic.

"Jesus, you're not a Rockette without a mike!" he hollered over me, grabbing for a bottle of Tylenol. "Bring it down a notch, will ya?"

Between Candace and me, I secretly considered myself the far better singer. Her voice was, although lovely, somewhat thin and soft, and I worried about her ability to impress a vocal coach whose pedigree included the career of a celebrity meteorologist.

But to my astonishment, barely three scales in, we were both accepted into study with Leonard. Perhaps, I thought, he saw such potential in the tall, charismatic baritone that he decided to accept the pretty but lesser blonde in order to snag a prized pupil.

Or perhaps it was something else.

"Twenty bucks a week, payable monthly, in advance," he barked. "I prefer cash."

• • •

"Sweetheart," I heard Leonard holler at Candace as I sat in the tiny waiting room outside the studio, "are you singing or farting? Get your voice out of your ASS!"

Leonard employed a variety of instructional techniques in his training, most of which involved a sort of semisupportive humiliation.

"Jesus," he would mutter as he withdrew a lozenge from his ever-present tin of Sucrets, "did you eat a block of brie before you came in here? You've got more phlegm than a rabbi at Seder."

"Diaphragms aren't just for whoring around, you know. Breathe!"

"I know you think your singing is candy for the ears, but it's giving me diabetes."

Although tact was in short supply, Leonard's coaching pushed us to new vocal heights. Candace was soon belting like the Wilson sisters from Heart (if they had emphysema), and I was extending my range into notes normally reserved for those who've been kicked repeatedly in the nuts.

• • •

Several months passed as Leonard and I labored at my craft. I whiled away my nonsinging hours dreamily perusing the catalogs of New York performing arts schools as I sat at the self-service gas station kiosk, yelling, "Pay first!" into a microphone.

I imagined sauntering into the school's professional-grade theater, high-fiving my new performer friends as they marveled at the skill with which I'd held the audience in the palm of my hand the previous night as Jesus Christ, Superstar. (Although, I mused, the character's unflattering hair would need to be rethought. Maybe a mullet.)

I had not yet garnered the courage to audition for another local musical, fearing that if I didn't get the lead, it would be viewed as an abject failure by those around me—most of whom, like Mother and Dad, continued to bang the drum for a backup plan.

"Just learn a marketable skill," Dad said. "Carpentry. Typing. Anything. We're not really up for supporting you until you need hemorrhoid cream."

Perish the thought. Although I loved my parents, spending the rest of my life dealing with Mother's inability to allow any-thing in the kitchen pantry beyond a box of Lucky Charms and a jar of peanut butter held little appeal. ("If we kept food in there," she had once explained helpfully, "I'll be tempted to eat it.")

"Well," I said to Dad, "carpentry is out." Although I had sat on a box in the garage as a child, watching him build all manner of useful yet tacky home furnishings, the intensity with which I had busied myself recounting the plotlines of *Bewitched* and *Here's Lucy* episodes precluded the ability to retain any new information.

Typing was also a nonstarter. I had never taken typing in high school, opting instead for a frantic hunt-and-peck system that, while impressive in its volume as I banged on the keys, resulted in the need for gallons of Wite-Out.

"Well, figure something out," Dad replied. "I'd like to retire at least twenty-four hours before I wake up dead."

• • •

"Do you think I should have a backup plan?" I asked Leonard one evening as I stood before the baby grand piano in his studio.

He sat back and looked at me, his thick, small hands resting atop his potbelly. There was silence for a long moment.

Finally, he spoke.

"Do you think you'll die if you don't get to spend your life performing?"

I wasn't entirely sure what the correct answer to this was, but after ruminating for a moment, I hesitantly opted for, "Yes...?"

"Do you want it more than anything else in the world? More than food? More than breathing?"

Now I saw where he was going with this. *Well*, I thought to myself, careful not to let any hesitation register on my face, *I think I do. It's not like I have a lot of other creative options at this point.*

"Yes," I replied. "Yes!"

"Good." He paused for a moment and gazed at me. "Why don't you come over for dinner Friday night and we'll figure out a game plan. It's not like I can leave it up to you. You're kind of retarded."

I was shocked. And thrilled. Candace had never been invited to Leonard's house. Clearly, this was an indication of a sort of star-pupil status.

"I'll be there!" I said excitedly. "What can I bring?"

"Your parents got any wine?"

• • •

I arrived at Leonard's charming, two-story home right on time, trembling with anticipation. Perhaps this dinner would be the first of dozens, I thought. With Leonard as my personal friend and mentor, the sky was the limit.

Leonard opened the door. "I'm just finishing the appetizers. Come on in."

I handed him the bottle of wine I had stolen from Mother and Dad's stash. Now that Val was married and I was just two years from legal drinking age, they had finally begun to trust their children and stopped locking the booze cabinet.

"Thanks." He retreated to the kitchen and I wandered into the living room, unsure whether to follow him. As Ella Fitzgerald played on the stereo, I glanced around. The decor reminded me of my grandmother's apartment in Kansas City—very matronly, with floral chintz and hints of lavender and rose. It didn't seem to fit with his brusque personality at all.

Leonard returned with a water goblet. "Glad you brought white," he said, filling the glass nearly to the rim. "We're having fish." As if these were somehow related. I nodded politely. This was all so adult.

"Let's go out back," he said, leading me through the house to a cozy backyard that included a small concrete patio. We sat down in webbed deck chairs across from each other. It was a beautiful evening, and I marveled at my good fortune, having a vocal coach who was so invested in my future.

"You have a beautiful home," I said. "Does your mother live here with you?"

"No, why?"

• • •

Dinner progressed somewhat stiltedly. We had discussed various musicals, and, in excruciating detail, Leonard's friendship with the celebrity meteorologist, but we were two hours into the evening and had yet to discuss my career or any next steps to stardom.

To calm my nerves a bit, I had begun gulping the wine like it was being served in a paper bag next to a dumpster. Both the room and Leonard were developing a pleasantly blurry edge.

"Well, someone certainly is thirsty," Leonard said, topping off my glass again, this time with a smile.

I had never seen Leonard smile. It felt oddly creepy, like a dog baring his fangs. *But this,* I reminded myself, *is the smile of a man who thinks I am an artist.*

"So, yeah," I said, gathering my courage, "about that game plan. Do you think I'm ready to audition for Juilliard?"

"You're getting there," he said dismissively. He suddenly sat up, becoming more animated. "Why don't you tell me something I don't know about Eric Poole. You know, like… a secret or something."

"Secret. A sheecret," I said, tipsily searching my data bank for anything that could be considered a juicy tidbit. "I don't really have any sheecrets." I jumped up. "How about if I jussst do the number I was thinking of doing for my audition?"

I started to sing "On a Clear Day," the Barbra Streisand song that had begun my theatrical career. This song held a special place in my heart now, and it felt like a full-circle moment to make it the song that might win me a place in a famed school for the performing arts.

I snapped my fingers with my right hand and did a stylish jazz hand with my left. Leonard's mouth dropped open. As I finished the line, "And you'll see who... you are," I did a snazzy three-quarter turn and pretended to tilt an imaginary top hat with my jazz hand.

"Oh, for God's sake," Leonard barked.

I stopped, shocked at his change in tone.

"When you do an audition, just stand there and sing. Interpret the song. Don't add a bunch of fucking choreography. You're not Tommy Tune."

His words stung. *I* am *Tommy Tune*, I thought, a bit drunkenly. *And Shirley MacLaine. I'm a hybrid of the theatrical superstars who have inspired me.* Why couldn't he see that?

This was the Leonard I knew. Harsh. Short-tempered. I was foolish to have expected more from him.

"Do you like movies?" Leonard said suddenly, changing the subject.

"Sure," I replied, still hurt by his curtness.

He pushed his chair back from the dinner table. "I have lots of them upstairs. Why don't we go watch one?"

He grabbed a bottle of wine and led me upstairs to the master bedroom. The bedroom was as dainty and girlish as the rest of the house, with a fainting couch in one corner and chandelier wall sconces. I noticed that a film projector was set up over the headboard of the bed, with a screen at the foot.

"How do you get copies of movies?" I said, trying to shake off my wounded feelings. He liked me, right? He clearly saw *something* special in me. "Do you know Martin Scorsheezzy?"

"Not exactly," he said with an odd giggle. He picked up the bottle. "More wine?"

"Sure."

He turned on the projector. Two men began riding horses, shirtless.

Ugh, a Western, I thought. The only reason I ever watched *Gunsmoke* when I was a little kid was for Miss Kitty. She was sassy.

"Do you like it?" Leonard said in a strangely husky voice, looking at the screen, then at me.

"Well," I slurred, "I tend to prefer comedies. You know, *Nine to Five, Airplane*. I like intelligent comedy, like *Cheech and Chong 2*, not that *Caddyshhhack* crap."

I looked back up at the screen. The men had ridden up to a corral and dismounted. Snooze. I refilled my wine glass.

Then, to my horror, the men began a process of remounting.

But not the horses.

My eyes grew as big at the grainy close-ups of these cowboys' anatomies.

"Good, huh? You like that?" There was that weird, throaty voice again. Suddenly, in a move Leonard had obviously performed enough times to perfect, he leaned over and unzipped my fly.

"Oh. No," I stammered. "Uh, no, I…" I pushed his open mouth, which had taken direct aim at my nearly exposed private parts, away from my jeans and sat up.

"You know you want it."

I stared at the dirty movie, at a loss as to how Leonard had decided that this was in any way appropriate post-dinner entertainment.

"No, I don't think I do…"

"Just relax," Leonard said hoarsely, pushing me back down on the bed, "and let Daddy take care of this." He grabbed for my zipper again.

"No!" I said, sitting up. "Nothing needs taking care of. I am perffffectly fine!"

It was, in this moment, unclear whether this sudden turn of events upset me because Leonard was a man, or because he was forty and kind of gross. What was clear was that I needed to get the hell out of there.

"Stop being a little tease," he said with what appeared to be bemusement.

"I'm not being a tease!" I hollered. "I am not *queer*."

Leonard sat up and pointed to my crotch. "Your hoo-ha begs to differ."

I jumped off the bed and zipped my fly. "I thought I was coming here to talk about my talent! Not get molested by my mentor."

"Mentor?" Leonard scoffed. "I'm your voice teacher. You pay me. And frankly, it's money down a giant shithole, if you ask me."

His words stopped me in my tracks.

"What?" I said, enraged. "You told me I have a great voice!"

"I lied," Leonard said evenly, swinging his legs over the side of the bed to sit up. "You have a very nice voice. You'll do well in community theater. But," he said, grabbing the pockets of my jeans and pulling me toward him again, "you'll *never* be a star." He began to unzip my pants again. "So you might as well learn who you are and just go with it." His face plunged into my crotch.

"This," I said, yanking away from him and grabbing my shoes from the floor, "will *never* be who I am!"

I ran down the stairs and out the front door, my shoes still in my hands, my head whirling with alcohol and disillusionment.

I jumped in the car and took off, driving a few blocks to ensure that Leonard would think I was gone, and then pulled over.

I was too intoxicated to drive. And I was crying.

There I sat, a nineteen-year-old man, bawling like an eight-year-old, unable to discern what it was I was mourning the most: the loss of an identity I had idealized, or a future that was filled with sin, and loneliness, and attempts to seduce innocent young men who dream of a bigger life.

···· Chapter 8 ····

THE LETTER

"Oh my GOD!"

My girlfriend Allison held up the ring, a marquis-shaped ruby encircled by stunning pavé cubic zirconias, as tears formed in her frosted-blue-eye-shadowed eyes.

"Yes! Oh, yes!" She hugged me tightly.

I was alternately delighted and mystified by her response. She obviously liked her Christmas present, but I hadn't asked her anything. As I began wondering what question she could possibly be answering, she flew up the stairs.

"I have to tell Mom!"

Abby Martin, a brassy combination of Mama Rose and Ma Kettle, who farted at meals and made announcements like, "I'm saving myself for my fifth husband" (in front of her fourth), was Allison's mother. Bawdy, liberal, and rich, thanks to a thriving medical practice and good divorce lawyers, she was a fiftyish blond who was built like a buxom linebacker.

And she was unlike any maternal figure I had ever met. She had kept the surname of husband number two, wisely figuring that, by number three, all bets were off.

I heard squeals from across the house. "Get your ass in here, mister!"

I proudly marched into the kitchen, where Abby, Allison, and her sister, Alyssa (who had been born with no sense of smell, a blessing in disguise given that her mother regularly let one fly during dinner), stood applauding. I had saved up for this ruby ring (an extraordinary half-carat total weight) for months, and I basked in the glow of their approval.

Since Leonard's devastating words a year earlier, I had abandoned all belief in my abilities as a performer. If someone of his caliber could deliver such a scathing critique, it seemed quite clear that I was deluding myself.

I was not a star.

I was not special.

The white-hot glow of the spotlight had never been meant to shine upon me.

This realization had led me to the cheerless conclusion that my entire journey of artistic and personal discovery had been a sham. And that if I was going to emulate anyone, it should be my beloved father, who worked in corporate America and had two children and led a life so utterly responsible and self-sacrificing and virtuous that it was a wonder he hadn't killed us all in our sleep.

This was, of course, anything but my ideal. In fact, it was my worst nightmare. But the years of mostly failing, of being good yet never quite good enough, had taken their toll.

I was tired of risking. A life like Dad's was, at least, safe—free from the judgments and the crushing disappointments that the pursuit of stardom had entailed.

So, this, I had decided, would be my quest now: a life of normalcy and routine. I would get a job. And, eventually, a family. As such, I had cut my college courses down to part-time and begun working full-time at a corporate travel agency. At TravelNation, I would build a stable, safe, colorless career. I would be doing not only what was right, but what God and my parents and, clearly, the world at large wanted for me. I only hoped that, as the years progressed, I would manage to mine some sort of creative joy from this sparkle-free existence.

I had also begun dating Allison, a fellow employee at the travel agency. Beautiful and amazingly kind, she had—albeit unknowingly—helped me to rechart the course of my life. In three to five years, I figured, we would get married and have some rug rats—children who would, perhaps, be able to live the life I had once dreamed of living.

Abby grabbed me and hugged me tightly, rocking back and forth as she began to cry. I knew that she adored me, as I did her, for she treated me like one of the family. (When Allison and I had sex in Allison's downstairs bedroom, Abby would throw open the door at the top of the stairs and scream, "Go, team!")

But this reaction to Allison's Christmas present, albeit an expensive gift, seemed over-the-top even for her. What was I supposed to do, I wondered? Bow? Curtsy? Pass around a tip jar?

"What do you think about the Westborough Country Club?" Abby said, handing me a glass of Asti Spumante.

"Well," I replied, "I'm not really dressed for it, but maybe they have a clip-on tie I can borrow?"

"I mean for the reception."

"Reception?"

Suddenly, the reason for her tears hit me, and I stood there, mute, a deer trapped in the headlights of an oncoming faux pas, unsure of an appropriate response. Abby's husband, whom we simply referred to as Four, had been absent for a couple of weeks. I'd been told he was on a business trip, but clearly something else was going on. Abby and Four must be through, I thought, and she's already planning a reception for her marriage to a new husband, Number Five.

"Sounds great. I've never been to a country club," I replied, determined to put a good face on Abby's latest matrimonial mishap. "Maybe I can catch the garter."

Alyssa snorted. "Uh, that probably wouldn't be a good idea."

"Yeah," Allison chuckled. "We wouldn't wanna start our life with a bad omen."

My smile froze.

"Just because I had some starter marriages doesn't mean *you* should," Abby added. She pulled out a photo album and opened it to pictures of a lodge-like home. "You can honeymoon at my brother's vacation house in Lake Tahoe. Isn't it gorgeous? Six bedrooms, two hot tubs, indoor pool. It's so big you need Sherpa guides."

I felt dizzy. And nauseous. I had somehow climbed aboard a runaway train, and Abby was driving.

• • •

I called my friend Kurt.

"Cheers, queer, what's up?"

In the couple of years since the Phillip incident, Kurt had somehow decided that I was suppressing my true self and now felt obliged to start every conversation with this greeting, which—as a good Christian—I was constantly called upon to forgive.

"I think I'm getting married," I whispered, so that Mother and Dad wouldn't hear.

"What!" He dropped the phone. "Hold, please," he bellowed from a distance, "your call is very important to us." He fished around and picked up the receiver. "Don't even kid about that. You just about gave me a coronary, and girl, I'm too young to die."

"Stop doing that *girl* thing."

"So, who's the unsuspecting bride?"

"Allison. Who else?"

"Oh… my… God!" he barked in his best Valley girl imitation. "How did this happen?" He paused. "Ohhhh, it was that *ring*."

"Yeah."

"It was just nice enough to qualify. Although who has a ruby engagement ring is beyond me, but hey, there's no accounting for taste."

"It was just supposed to be a Christmas gift. I mean, I love Allison…"

"And I love Toaster Strudel, but that doesn't mean I want to screw it."

"I have sex with her all the time," I said defensively.

"Yeah, after a bottle of booze. Do the math."

"What am I gonna do? I'm not ready to get married."

"Well, you're not getting any younger," he replied. "Or straighter."

Forgiveness was exhausting.

"You have to tell her the truth," he said. "And fast, before they start taking measurements for the straitjacket."

I desperately wanted Kurt to come over and commiserate, but since I still lived at home, this was not an option. His tragic inability to hide who he was meant that he could never meet Mother and Dad.

I hung up the phone and lay on the bed, my mind racing. As a B. R. Tibbits tape on the sanctity of marriage blared through the house—"Marriage is a contract that must not be dishonored. The holy bond of right man and right woman is unseverable"—I began to imagine how the coming events would unfold.

Since we currently had no money, we would live in her basement bedroom, saving our pennies to one day rent our own place, a dingy third-floor walk-up in a south city neighborhood for which the term *urban blight* had thought-fully been coined. Allison would quit work to raise our two screaming children, and I would surrender to alcoholism and bitterness.

"Please, God," I pleaded quietly, desperately. "Save me."

Suddenly, it occurred to me: although I knew that I had no real options outside of mimicking the life of my father, per-haps the problem was that Allison wasn't my "right woman." As this thought raced across the landscape of possibilities, I recalled a moment some weeks before, when, in an effort to understand Kurt's lifestyle, I had allowed him to take me to a gay bar, Faces, located in a delightful area of East St. Louis best known for its crime rate.

As we sat in the parking lot drinking a box of Franzia white zinfandel, and I tried to summon the courage to go in, I had asked him a question.

"So, how do you know when you're gay?"

He thought about this for a long moment. Finally, peering thoughtfully out the window at the nightclub, as though counting the commandments that were being broken inside, he replied with great conviction, "You get a letter."

"Some people's letter," he explained, "comes FedEx. For others, it arrives third class. Some people read the whole letter right away. Others read a paragraph, then put it in a drawer. Some people's letters are long and complicated. Others just say, 'Welcome to the club.'"

What was I most worried about, I thought, as I turned this conversation over and over in my mind: that Allison wasn't my right woman? That my dad's life wasn't, somehow, the life I really wanted? Or that I had gotten a letter?

• • •

Bridal magazines were scattered across the den. Abby and Allison lay on the floor, a bottle of Asti between them, as Abby scoured the pages for ideas. I sat in a wing chair, refusing the liquor, nervously twisting my class ring as I gazed at Allison with conflicted feelings of love and fear, adoration and resentment.

She was a crystal blue–eyed brunette who struggled with her weight—dazzling when thin, "the girl with the pretty face" when plumper. But what truly made her beautiful was her kindness, her generosity, her ability to love and accept all the quirks of the young man who worshipped her.

"Mom, we don't need to decide all this right now," Allison protested. "We haven't even set a date yet."

You haven't even been asked *yet,* I thought to myself.

"A date's the easy part," Abby replied. "Picking a dress—that's hard."

"You think it's okay if I wear white?" Allison queried.

"Hell, yeah," Abby answered. "Listen, if I'd done color gradations, I'd be on charcoal now."

Kurt's admonition rang in my head. I took a deep breath. "Hey, Allison… you wanna go for a walk?"

We strolled down the leafy suburban block, hand in hand, as I gazed up at the eighty-year-old trees shading the majestic homes of this wealthy community. My family's North County neighborhood was a middle-class tract home development with four ranch styles, which made finding the bathroom at a friend's house a snap since you knew all the layouts by heart. Allison's West County world of custom-built homes and Cadillacs felt like a far cry from the life I had led, and I had to admit that it was intoxicating. Had I stayed in this relationship because of that?

"Is everything okay?" Allison asked.

"Well, I just need to tell you something."

"Actually," she replied, looking me in the eye, "me, too."

I nearly gasped. *Maybe she feels it, too! Maybe this is too much for her, as well. Maybe she has been trying to please Abby and doesn't really want to marry me, either—or at least, not yet.*

"My mom has absolutely lost her shit. I've gotta reel her in."

A tidal wave of relief washed over me. "So you think this is all happening too fast, too?"

"Yeah," she replied, squeezing my hand.

I wanted to dance across the well-manicured lawns. *Thank you, Jesus.*

"She's trying to make all the decisions for us. I mean, you probably want to have some input, right? This is your wedding, too." She smiled her dazzling smile. "I think *you* should pick the color of the tuxes. What do you think, powder blue or sky blue?"

The sparkle in her eyes did me in.

• • •

When we returned, Abby was waiting, drink in hand. "Let's talk music for the reception."

A lengthy discussion of Hall & Oates cover bands ensued, or so I assumed; I was far too busy mentally assessing the pros and cons of the witness protection program or possibly a fiery car crash.

Gradually, my stomach began to churn, bile rising in my throat. I felt the salty thickening of the glands that precedes the involuntary eviction of the contents of one's stomach. I jumped to my feet.

"I, I… I don't feel good. I'm gonna go."

I flew toward the front door as Allison and Abby looked up, confused. Before they could say a word, I was gone.

I jumped into the car and drove several blocks before throwing open the car door in anticipation of what would come next. But no evacuation ensued. My hands shook as I gripped the red vinyl steering wheel of my Chevy Malibu, sweat pouring down my face.

Then, out of the corner of the rearview mirror, I spotted

something lying in the backseat—a bottle of Asti that Allison had purchased. Champagne. Carbonated. Good for the tummy. I grabbed the bottle and popped the cork, gulping down some of the sugary liquid as I began whispering once again, "Save me."

As a child, when I made magical requests, I had been filled with visions of what could be. What I truly believed *would* be. But now, no visual came to mind. I could picture no alternate reality.

Fortunately, within moments, the alcohol began to calm my nerves. My focus became fuzzy around the edges, and the world seemed slightly less bleak. Finally, I started the car and headed toward the highway, my brain swimming in serotonin. *It'll be okay*, I told myself. *Think positively. You'll find a way through this.*

I thought of the letter Kurt had referred to. "Dear Prospective Member," it would probably begin. "You may not have been expecting this missive, but it was not sent to you by mistake."

Suddenly, I realized that I was headed the wrong direction on the highway—40 East took me into downtown St. Louis. Into the bad neighborhoods. Where the gay bars were.

I didn't turn around.

● ● ●

In half an hour, I had somehow found my way to Faces, a virtual miracle given my absence of any sense of direction (after three years, the layout of my college campus remained an exotic mystery). I sat outside the building, listening to the thumping music and gulping the Asti, as I watched young men leap from their cars and dash into the club to avoid getting hit by flying beer bottles or the occasional baseball bat.

"Why am I here?" I said aloud as I stared at the flashing disco lights dulled by the bar's dark-tinted door. "There's nothing for me in this place." I unbuttoned two more buttons on my shirt.

Finally summoning the courage, I jumped out of my car and ran toward the door, waving wildly to draw the attention of the bouncer out front, who conveniently doubled as a witness in assault trials.

I entered the club intact and was immediately assaulted instead by the pounding music and a thick haze of smoke. I recalled the high-tech decor from my brief visit with Kurt some weeks earlier. I had to admit, this place was nicer than the straight clubs Allison and I patronized. Who knew sinning could be so stylish.

"That'll be two dollars, toots."

I looked up to find the same tiny, seventy-year-old woman sitting behind the cash register who had been there previously. Her mousy perm and Members Only windbreaker swathed a bag of skin that resembled a Louis Vuitton handbag. She blew large, impressive smoke rings as she held out her palm.

I paid the cover charge and crept into the club, glancing quickly around to see if anyone recognized me and was calling the papers. Fortunately, it was only nine forty-five and pretty much the only other people there were some straight girls whose bachelorette party had taken an interesting turn.

Faces was, in essence, a homosexual theme park, a Disneyland of depravity. The main floor was a large discotheque, the second floor, a drag club. The basement hosted a seedy pool table bar and a long, narrow, pitch-black room that Kurt euphemistically referred to as the "Tunnel of Love."

As the Pointer Sisters' "Jump" shook the walls, I stepped up to the bar. More liquid courage would be necessary.

"Screwdriver, please!" I screamed to the bartender.

He poured a tall glass of rotgut vodka with a splash of OJ for color and slid it in front of me. I stepped to the side, unsure where to stand in the empty, cavernous club, posing awkwardly in an ill-conceived attempt to look alluring.

As I began to gulp the drink down, trying not to choke on the medicinal taste, I realized that the half bottle of Asti was now awaiting an exit strategy. I slunk unobtrusively over to the restroom and opened the door.

I had never seen a men's room quite like this. There were mirrors. Lots of mirrors. And an appalling lack of privacy. The door on the one stall didn't lock, and the urinals had been replaced by a single long trough that made it seem like you were peeing in the kitchen sink. Thank God no one else was in here, I thought as I sidled up to relieve myself.

Suddenly, the door whooshed open and someone stepped up next to me at the trough, effectively stopping my urination midstream. He nudged me.

Oh my God, I thought, *the predators are on me already!* Barely in the door, and I was chum in the waters of deviance.

"Well, well, well… if it isn't the bride-to-be."

I turned to find Kurt standing next to me. He was wearing Brittania jeans, a see-through mesh jacket from J.C. Penney, and a straw fedora with a blue polka-dot sash.

"What brings you here?" he asked. "Doing a documentary on denial?"

"I was, um, going to meet Allison at a bridal shop, and I got lost." I mentally congratulated myself on my quick thinking as I crossed to the sink to avoid his stare.

"What bridal shop is open at this hour?" he replied. "This isn't Vegas. Although God knows some of the brides in this town would look better in the dark. Or under a craps table."

He gazed seductively at himself in the mirror as if under the impression that he was the hottest thing in the club. Fortunately, since it was only us and a pack of drunk straight girls, his odds were decent. He threw open the door and struck a pose that he had obviously picked up from Richard Gere in *American Gigolo*. One of the bachelorette girls winked at him.

He elbowed me. "Did you see that? I am on *fire!*"

He turned to grab his drink as the girl in question staggered off the dance floor and vomited into her Long Island iced tea.

As one of her friends hustled her off to the ladies' room, a stream of young men suddenly began pouring into the club.

"What's the deal?" I shouted as guys practically trampled one another to get in the door. "Did the bus let off?"

"The cover goes up at ten o'clock," Kurt replied as he pulled me into a corner. "So… you got lost and ended up at this den of iniquity. Why'd you come inside?" He motioned to the upstairs drag club with a smirk. "Most of the brides in here are baritones."

Whether it was the liquor kicking in or my exhaustion at having to lie, I decided, for once, to try the truth. "I don't know."

His smirk faded. He patted my hand. "Come on," he bellowed as Laura Branigan's "Gloria" began to rock the building. "Let's show these real girls how it's done."

He started to pull me onto the dance floor. I was mortified. I had never danced with a guy before. Our last visit to Faces had consisted of thirty minutes of standing in a dark corner as I creatively attempted to shield my face with a bar napkin, fanning myself nervously until some guy inquired as to the whereabouts of my kimono.

"No, no, I just want to watch," I protested, but it was too late. Kurt yanked me into the middle of the floor. We were now the center of attention for the entire bar, since, for most of the patrons, the drunk and available straight girls were merely a mildly interesting but superfluous extra, like cottage cheese on a dessert buffet.

I began to dance, hesitantly, awkwardly, a mentally challenged Lurch with balance issues. Kurt immediately began a series of *Dance Fever* moves that made it look like he was being mildly electrocuted. It didn't seem to matter. The bachelorette party cheered us on, encircling us like a ring of hunters closing in on a pair of felled deer.

One of the girls slapped my butt playfully. "Whoo!" she shrieked, high-fiving her friends as if she had just scored a touchdown at the Super Bowl. The alcohol was removing my inhibitions, and in response, I began to shake my groove thing like a tambourine at a Village People concert, to the delight of the women—as well as a couple of men, who smiled shyly.

"Gay guys are so much fun!" another girl screamed before falling off her heels.

By the time Irene Cara's "What a Feelin'" began booming through the speakers, a dozen other couples had swept onto the dance floor. It was officially a party. Kurt and I shimmied across the room in a giddy haze, drinking in the attention.

He did a Carol Merrill arm sweep. "See what you're missing?"

"Yeah!" I hollered. "I didn't know girls came to places like this! I should bring Allison!"

• • •

The next morning, I lay in my bedroom, hungover yet exhilarated, my ear still ringing. I had never been so drunk with freedom. I had never been so drunk with possibility. I had never been so drunk.

Then I thought again of the letter. "Dear Prospective Member," it would probably continue, "we urge you to read on…"

• • •

That night, the phone rang.

Dad, who was de-icing the dresser in their frostbitten master bedroom, answered it. I heard him holler to Mother, who was in the shower. "Elaine? It's Allison's mother, Abby."

I leaped out of bed as though shot from a Barnum and Bailey cannon.

Mother and Dad had never met Abby. On purpose. Mother's penchant for giving social introductions the festive tenor of hostage negotiations had kept her and Dad from meeting Allison for nearly a year. (Ironically, when they did meet, Mother couldn't have been more welcoming, which made me wonder if her past moodiness had simply been the result of a particularly lengthy menopause of, say, sixteen years.)

But Abby was something else altogether. Abby was liberal.

And profane. And most importantly, Abby was likely to spill the beans.

I knocked politely on the door and, throwing caution to the wind, didn't even wait for an answer. I threw open the door as a blast of cold air hit me in the face. Mother was on the phone. Her eyes sparkled.

"Well, that sounds lovely. Yes, it certainly would be nice if we met"—she elbowed Dad excitedly—"before the *wedding*. Two weeks from Saturday? That sounds lovely."

She hung up the phone and turned to Dad.

"Praise the Lord!"

A level of hosannas and glad tidings ensued that should have signaled the second coming. Our family was not fond of physical contact, but Mother threw her arms around me and Dad even piled on. I could not have made them happier had I voted for the death penalty.

"This calls for a celebration!" Mother declared. "Ray, get the Mateus!"

• • •

I called Kurt.

"Ohmigod, ohmigod, now Mother and Dad know."

"I could be wrong," he replied calmly as he slurped his Coke, "but wouldn't they find out eventually, like when they're throwing rice on you outside the church?"

"But now I can't…"

"Can't what?"

I didn't respond.

"You can't stop it?"

"I can't let everybody down," I replied, my words tumbling

out. "Mother and Dad are so excited. Allison's so excited. Abby's so…"

"Yeah, I get it. The whole world is united. Kumbaya." His voice echoed as he downed the last drops. "You gotta stop worrying about what everybody else thinks."

"I don't care what other people think."

"Eric," he replied, chuckling, "you double-book with different friends on Saturday nights because you don't want to disappoint anybody. You let the car salesman sell you undercoating, rustproofing, and fabric protection because you didn't want him to think you were cheap. When I ask you if a pair of jeans makes me look fat, you never tell me yes."

"Is it so wrong to be nice?"

"It is if I look like an overinflated blow-up doll."

"My dad is the nicest person I've ever known. I could do worse than to be like him."

"Maybe you should try just being you."

"Yeah, well," I said, "that hasn't gone so great."

There was a long pause.

"I feel like I'm drowning," I said.

"Well, that's natural," Kurt replied. "Anybody'd be nervous about making the biggest mistake of their life."

"It's not a mistake! I just don't know if I want to have my dad's life. I mean… yet."

"So when *will* you be ready to make this mistake?"

"It's not a *mistake!*"

"Then why are you so panicked?"

I had no answer. Or, at least, none I could say aloud.

"Congratulations," he said, popping the top on another can. "Looks like you're finally reading your letter."

• • •

I retreated to my bedroom.

I knelt in front of my bed, imagining my eight-year-old self in full magical regalia, mightily commanding the universe. Changing the world at my whim. Making it simpler. Kinder. More organized.

I pictured a world where God didn't care who anyone loved. Where I could tell people the truth and not fear their reactions. Where I had the courage to become the person *I* most wanted to be, not the person everyone else expected me to be. I pictured a world that I still, somehow, in the tiniest corner of my soul, believed was possible.

And I picked up a pen.

• • •

"Dear Allison," the letter began. "I'm so sorry to do this by mail instead of telling you face-to-face, but this seemed like the kindest way to do it. I know your reaction may be shock, so I wanted to give you the time to deal with it privately."

I took a moment to congratulate myself on my thoughtfulness and deep concern for her feelings, then continued to write.

"There's someone else. We just met recently. I'd rather not say who, and really, I guess in the scheme of things it doesn't matter, anyway. It took me by surprise, just as this note has probably done to you. But I have to pursue it, which means that now I must let you go so that I can see where it leads.

"I have loved our time together. You are an amazing woman and someone I will always hold close to my heart. I hope that, in time, we can be friends. I realize that may not happen for several months, but I'm willing to wait."

"Love, Eric."

• • •

Immediately upon receiving the letter, Allison took a leave of absence at the travel agency. And the women I worked with took sides.

One side.

"How could you do this?"

"And by a letter? Are you *kidding* me?"

"Who is this slut?"

"Where did you meet her?"

"How could something like this just happen out of the blue when you're engaged?"

"Were you cheating on her?"

"You're a pig."

"You're a jerk."

"Typical *man*."

I had told Allison there was "someone else" because I was terrified that she would try to talk me out of this. And that I would be weak enough to allow her to. But no matter how I tried to frame it, within myself or to others, there was no escaping the facts: what I had done was cowardly. Unforgivably cruel. And a big, fat, ugly lie.

My coworkers issued ongoing bulletins of Allison's condition.

"All she does is cry."

"And drink Asti Spumante."

"And play 'Tainted Love' over and over."

"She hasn't eaten in two weeks."

"She's lost fifteen pounds."

"She's practically Karen Carpenter. If she ends up dead over a toilet, it'll be on your head."

I was a terrible person. And I hated myself for devastating this beautiful, sensitive girl who had never done anything but love me.

Yet, even within my mortification and shame, I was incredibly, monumentally relieved. A tremendous weight had been lifted from my shoulders. For the first time in my life, I felt free. I felt as if I had done the best thing for both of us. As if, somehow, in doing so, I had discovered the me I was meant to be.

And suddenly, it seemed as though God had led me to this decision; that, even more than being straight, more than being my father, he wanted me to be honest. That projecting my truth out into the world was the only way to discover who I truly, authentically was.

• • •

Of course, one issue still remained: I had to tell Mother and Dad. And fast. Dinner at Abby's was now three days away.

I lay on my bed, conjuring excuses.

Allison was dead.

No.

She'd been committed.

No.

She was a Satanist.

No, but interesting.

She hated kids. She wanted us to live in a commune. Her

mother's medical practice was a front for a Colombian drug cartel.

No. No. Also interesting.

George Michael had met Allison at a concert and asked her to marry him.

Hmm. That one had potential.

It was Thursday night, and the mood around the house had been unusually festive for the past couple of weeks. Tonight, the heat was cranked up to sixty-two, Mother had consumed an entire half cup of lima bean casserole (a banquet compared to her usual meal of decaf and a breath mint), and we had placed the dirty dishes right into the dishwasher as though we used it all the time. Mother was scrubbing the sink and Dad was Dustbusting the stove hood fan when I finally worked up the nerve.

"Mother, Dad," I said loudly, "I have something to tell you."

Their backs stiffened. As if someone had flipped a switch, I could feel the tenor of the room change. Mother and Dad glanced at one another as Dad switched off the Dustbuster and Mother set down the can of Comet. They turned around slowly, obviously afraid my head might be spinning or I would be eating a small child.

Mother grabbed Dad's arm. "What happened?" The sense of dread in her voice was so odd given that she had no idea what was coming.

"Allison and I broke up."

"Dear God, no," Dad whimpered, almost before I got the words out. Of course, I shouldn't have been surprised at his reaction. He and Mother thought the world of her.

"Why?" Mother said plaintively, her voice quaking. "What did you do?"

"I didn't do anything!" I said defensively. I turned away from them. Their eyes seemed to be boring holes into my skull, and I was certain they could read my thoughts. "We're just not right for each other."

"So how is it," Dad said, "that you figured this out *after* you asked her to marry you?"

"I didn't ask her to marry me!" I protested. "It was all a big misunderstanding!"

"Well, why *don't* you want to marry her?"

Was God providing me an opening, an opportunity to share my angst, my fears, my *truth* with the parents who had loved and raised and only wanted the best for me provided it fell within the guidelines of the church?

"Ray..." Mother said quickly, "Ray, don't."

"Well, to be honest..." I took a deep breath. This was my moment. My hands were shaking so hard that I had to shove them into my pockets. "To be honest—"

"You're just not right for each other," Mother jumped in, finishing my sentence for me, a sense of finality in her tone that precluded argument. "And that's okay. You'll find someone else."

"That's right," Dad jumped in. "Sometimes you have to kiss a few frogs before you meet your prince."

"*Princess*, Ray."

"Princess," he replied quickly. "Right. You know what I mean."

There was a long, uncomfortable pause. Mother turned to Dad.

"Ray…" she said quietly, "get the Mateus."

Chapter 9

THE BOY BOMBECK

"Eric, can I see you in my office?"

There was a loud, communal gasp. Sheila, the manager of TravelNation, the large corporate travel agency where I earned a paycheck merrily insulting my coworkers by inter-office computer—and also quality-controlling flight reservations—was summoning me.

No one left Sheila's office without mascara streaming down their face. Even the men.

Sheila did not call you into her dungeon to praise the quality of your work. No one knew exactly what went on in there, but it was rumored that she donned a latex bodysuit and stilettos and whipped you until you both cried.

Rumor quickly spread throughout the building, and as I slunk down the hall to her office, people lined the hallway, silently expressing their sympathies and offering whispered tips.

"Ask her to hit you where it won't show."

"Don't beg for mercy. It makes her madder."

This was so not how I had envisioned my life. Of course, at this point I really didn't *have* a vision for my life, except perhaps the homo part. Although I felt enormous relief and comfort in beginning to accept the fact that I was gay, I seemed to be no closer to finding my calling than when I was sixteen. Getting fired would just be added to the list of failures that had become my identity.

Joey, the IT guy for the company, elbowed one of the girls and laughed.

"Who didn't see this coming?"

Sheila's office door was open. As I stepped into it, she looked up.

"Come in. And close that behind you."

I wondered if the door hermetically sealed so that no one could hear the screams. I stood as close to it as possible, unsure whether it would even open if I tried to make a run for it.

"Well, *sit down.*" She motioned to the chairs in front of her desk.

Sheila was a tall, black-haired, and quite attractive woman in her forties, but in this moment, her features were not lit up by any form of warmth. *She's called me in to fire me over my computer-logged comments to other employees*, I thought. These merry insults, my attempts to amuse my fellow coworkers as we communicated back and forth about client reservations, were all in fun, even if they did occasionally cross the line of good taste.

I had been warned to knock it off, but I couldn't help myself. The days at TravelNation were long, arduous, and stressful.

I had begun in the reservations pool, taking flight reservations from corporate executives, many of whom clearly found conversing with travel agents akin to having their wives discover another woman's panties under the bed. And if you were unlucky enough to answer the call when they were on the road and something had gone awry, you got a barrage of language that would make a rapper blush.

The executives' assistants weren't much better: most seemed to feel that the phone would detonate if they remained on the line longer than thirty seconds. I would hear a stream of information screamed at DEFCON 4 levels, followed by a click. I imagined them in their offices, backing away from the phone, hands up, screaming, "Whoo! Clear!"

The job was, to put it mildly, stressful, repetitive, and boring. Fortunately, the modest—some might term it "sweeping"—attention to detail that I had inherited from Mother served me well here; only a year after joining the company, I had been promoted from reservations to the quality-control department. But this new position was even more mind-numbing, since all I did was sit there, painstakingly checking the work of other agents and daydreaming about being gunned down in a 7-Eleven.

I desperately needed a little amuse-bouche to get through the day. And until now, I had assumed that these electronically transmitted bons mots had brightened my fellow employees' days as well.

Sheila glanced down and began to read.

"I see you're wearing the same dress you left in last night. Congrats on another successful first date."

She looked up at me disapprovingly, then continued reading.

"Your body is like a children's playground—sticky, full of germs, and frequented by perverts."

She paused, as if waiting for some kind of response from me, but I didn't want to give her any more reason to don the stilettos.

"Your minister called," she read. "He'd like his ball gag back."

She leaned forward and stared at me. Should I defend myself, I wondered? Should I fall to my knees? I didn't want to lower my head in shame lest she produce the whip without my knowledge.

"These kind of comments," Sheila said, "are wildly inappropriate in a corporate setting. And these days, people sue."

I nodded.

"Eric," she said, "you're an excellent employee. You're a hard worker, you're committed, and you clearly love travel."

I did, indeed. Since my trip to New York several years earlier, I had dreamed of a glitzy life jet-setting around the world. And that was what had attracted me to the job: the opportunity to take advantage of "fam trips"—familiarization trips for travel agents, designed to acquaint them with an airline or hotel's product so they could recommend it to their clients. These trips—like a five-day jaunt to London with business-class air, four-star hotels, meals and tours for $199—were intoxicating. When some coworkers and I took this particular trip, an acquaintance had called the house while

I was gone, and, to my delight, Dad had said to her, "Sorry, he's in London." He also added, "Having dinner with a bunch of cats" (we were seeing the musical *Cats*). But I forgave him. It still sounded glamorous enough to make her hate me.

Sheila continued. "The fact that we value you made it that much harder to figure out what to *do* about this. Should we fire you, to set an example? Should we make you apologize in front of the entire company?"

She reclined in her high-backed executive chair as I stared down at the floor, imagining having to get up in front of the whole company to ask forgiveness. Joanne, a large, cantankerous woman who booked international trips and who was almost universally despised, would probably demand that I be flogged naked in front of her while she ate corn dogs.

There was a knock at the door.

"It's Tess."

Tess, another manager at the company sauntered into the room, closing the door behind her. Everyone liked her, and I was relieved to see her—perhaps, I thought, her presence would distract Sheila enough for me to escape before the whip comes out.

Tess was an attractive woman of about forty. Big-boned, with a big personality, her husband was a top St. Louis radio personality, and she didn't need this job.

"I don't know what you're doing working in travel," she said to me, chuckling, as she flopped down in the chair next to me. "You oughta be writing for Joan Rivers."

I almost gasped. I had an ally!

"You clearly need some sort of creative outlet," Sheila said with a note of disapproval in her voice.

"So, guess what?" Tess said excitedly. "We're starting a monthly newsletter that will go out to all the employees. And I thought that you should write a humor column for it."

I nearly fell off my chair.

"Now, let's be clear," Sheila said sternly. "This will be your form of expression going forward. No more inter-office insults."

"Yes, ma'am!" I replied excitedly.

"No more personal remarks of any kind in the reservation records."

"I promise."

"And keep it clean in this column, you got it?"

I nodded.

"I want to say congratulations," Sheila said as she rose to denote that our meeting was over, "but that would indicate some sort of tacit approval of your behavior. So, I'm sure you understand that I can't do that."

"I do. I do," I said as I backed out of the room. "Thank you!"

Tess turned so that Sheila couldn't see her face and winked at me.

Fairly glowing, I threw open the door.

Employees scattered like roaches. No one wanted to look at me, to see the tears in my eyes, the bloody flesh, the heel marks. But as I buzzed down the hall, humming happily, people began to realize that something was amiss.

"Why isn't he sobbing?"

"Maybe he's in shock."

Joey, the IT guy, who had never particularly liked me, caught up with me. "Don't worry"—he smirked—"you'll find another job. Every company needs a guy like you to make the women feel safe."

"What are you talking about?" I snapped, annoyed by his glee at my perceived firing. "I am about," I said haughtily, "to be *published*."

Since stumbling onto an Erma Bombeck book a few years earlier, I had become a huge fan of the woman who made family life funny. And although I had never endeavored to write actual humor pieces outside of a quickly aborted attempt at college, it now seemed as though others felt I had the ability to do so. I was being given a vote of confidence in a path that I had never really considered possible.

A wave of excitement washed over me. It suddenly seemed as if I was standing on the precipice of a whole new life. Maybe I *didn't* have to be my father. Maybe I *could* make a living in the creative arts.

Erma, I had read, earned million-dollar book advances. She did segments on *Good Morning America*. She made speeches around the country after which she was allowed to browse in a Brinks truck. Perhaps, I thought, I could become the male Erma Bombeck, writing amusing missives that would earn me the same sort of wealth and popularity.

Or at least enough to move out of the house.

Thank you, God, I said silently. I wasn't entirely sure how much he'd had to do with this, but it did somehow seem as if someone was directing this from above.

• • •

Within months, my stature at TravelNation began to grow a bit, as the staff eagerly anticipated each newsletter. Whether

out of a desperate need for something to brighten the inter-
minable workdays or the narcissistic hope that they would be
mentioned by name and thus earn a largely undeserved fifteen
minutes, my column was considered a highlight—a feat
accomplished by being the only amusing thing in a newsletter
filled with health-care updates and grim news about raises.

I quickly settled into writing about two travel-centric topics
that seemed to appeal to my readers. Since airline deregulation
a few years earlier, the friendly skies had become somewhat less
affable, given that flight attendant pay was becoming squeezed
and more and more seats were being shoved into planes. This
provided a wealth of material along the lines of "Wrapping Your
Legs Behind Your Ears: A Step-by-Step Guide" and "Flight
Attendants: Air Mattresses or War Criminals?"

The second topic centered around my own travels with
coworkers and included festive recounts of various humiliations,
like the time my friend Mindy and I paraded out of Harrods
department store in London, Mindy acting for all the world like
she was Bianca Jagger, and as she glanced up, a pigeon shit on
her face.

The attention I received was thrilling. As I was the only
person in the entire company who seemed to possess any sort
of flair for an amusing turn of phrase, everyone began to look
at me differently. Reservation agents and managers alike who,
prior to this, had barely seemed aware of my existence as a
humanoid form, began to corner me in the hallways with information that they hoped I would use as fodder for an upcoming
column.

"Karen and I were at Club Med in the Dominican
Republic last week," someone would whisper to me as if in

possession of enriched uranium and a list of third-world dictators, "and she got so drunk she passed out in a lounge chair. At 11:00 a.m."

"Talk about how we get all of these travel perks, but we can't afford to take advantage of them because we're paid like galley slaves," others would suggest, confusing me with Norma Rae.

"I won St. Louis Travel Agent of the Year, if you want to put that in your silly little byline," Joanne would snap, apparently under the impression that belittling my work was a surefire path to publicity.

This minor celebrity began to bolster my confidence, and slowly I began to believe that perhaps I *could* somehow become the Boy Bombeck. I imagined making appearances on the *Today* show in my weekly segment, "Traveling Light." I imagined becoming best friends with Jane Pauley and making fun of Gene Shalit's hair.

And for the first time since Leonard's damning words, I imagined myself as someone.

This newfound attention was not lost on Joey. He was an extremely good-looking twenty-four-year-old who, as the agency stud, basked in the glow of adoration from the many female employees. Tall and broad shouldered, with confidence to burn, Joey was everything I despised. And wanted to be.

I longed for the life of a studly straight guy, for whom everything came easily. But such was not to be. Although I had privately accepted my life path as a gay person, this acceptance did not extend to an open display of said lifestyle, since, as a general rule, I preferred not to be dragged behind a pickup. Suburban St. Louis was not Greenwich Village.

Thus, no one at TravelNation knew. And given the bomb-throwing words of our stereo-blasted minister, B. R. Tibbits, it was clear that my parents would also have to be kept in the dark, lest they be forced to burn a cross on their own lawn.

But, somehow, Joey seemed to suspect something, even though I did as little as possible to implicate myself as a homo. True, all my best friends at work were women. True, I loved Barbra Streisand and Diana Ross and daring fashion. True, the rules of football remained as inscrutable as the Chinese language.

But luckily, the women at TravelNation either didn't notice or they found putting two and two together unnecessarily arduous. Joey, on the other hand, was quick to decrypt these actions as the Morse Code of gayness. A gayness that seemed to become ever more irritating to him as my new-found fame began to steal a bit of the spotlight—a spotlight that was usually trained on Joey.

He began trying to catch me glancing his way. "What are you looking at?" he would snap. "You're creeping me out."

"I wasn't looking at *you*," I would retort, although actually I was, since 95 percent of the employees of TravelNation were women, and the other 5 percent were men who had little personal acquaintance with the term *underwear model*. "I was looking at… at that poster of Africa behind you. *I* appreciate unusual cultures."

"I'll *bet* you do."

Then, one morning, Sheila gathered everyone in the central reservations bullpen for an impromptu company meeting.

"I'm happy to inform you," she announced as she rotated steel balls in the palm of her hand, "that because our business is growing so rapidly, we are expanding to include an evening shift."

Polite applause and murmurs of "For this they called a meeting?" and "Ewww, I'm not working at night" filled the room.

"We're proud to appoint Eric Poole as manager of this shift. Lisa Reynolds will be reporting to him, and they'll be working from three to eleven. Let's all congratulate Eric on his well-deserved promotion."

People clapped politely, wondering if this was actually a promotion or a sentence, as I beamed. Joey joined a circle of congratulants, grabbing my hand to shake it warmly. I was taken aback at his geniality, and I smiled at him. Perhaps he was having second thoughts about his dickish behavior. Perhaps he recognized that there was nothing left to do but accept the fact that, at least occasionally, he might have to share the TravelNation spotlight with someone. He stepped next to me and leaned in close.

"You only got the job," he whispered, "because everybody else has a life."

Several days later, Sheila called me down to her office again.

"Just wanted to let you know that Joey is going to begin coming in midday," she announced, "so he'll be working alongside you and Lisa into the evening."

I blanched. One of the joys of this "promotion," such as it was, was the opportunity to escape being harassed by Joey for eight hours a day, and now that was being taken away from me before it had even begun.

But then, it occurred to me: *I* was the manager of the late shift.

"Hey," Joey hollered, catching up to me as I exited her office, "what did Captain Jewface want now?"

"She wanted to let me know that I have a new employee," I said gleefully, punching my finger into his broad, tanned chest. "YOU."

"Oh, yeah?" he replied. "We'll see about that!"

"You're in charge at night," Sheila informed me when Joey and I marched back into her office, demanding clarification, "but since Joey's in IT, you're not in charge of him."

• • •

"It's really great having you here with us," Lisa said to Joey, in a show of Judas-like support, as we all sat working. "Eric and I get kinda sick of each other."

This was more or less true, since Lisa liked sports and punk rock music and was shockingly unversed in the plotlines of *The Love Boat*. But Joey didn't need to be apprised of this.

"Who could get sick of *you*?" Joey said flirtatiously.

His voice was deep and rich and only served to underscore his charisma, a fact that he was irritatingly aware of, and Lisa hung on his every word as if he were Yoda with biceps.

"If I had an employee like you, I'd be tempted to just let her go shopping and gossip on the phone with her friends and dance naked around the office."

No one could accuse Joey of feminism.

"Of course," he added, "that's probably what Eric would like to do."

"Oh, stop," Lisa said half-heartedly as she appeared to bat her eyelashes at Joey. "Eric isn't a fag. He left Allison for another girl."

"You sure it was a girl?"

"Well, we haven't met her," Lisa replied, a sudden doubt coloring her voice.

Oblivious to the swiftly declining value of a joke repeated twice, Joey continued, "Eric, you wish you could dance naked for me, don't you?"

"I have better things to do with my time," I replied, attempting to type but only managing gibberish, "than to educate you on what a normal-size willy looks like."

"Sorry to hear you're just average down there," Joey said, winking at Lisa. "I wear a size-twelve shoe."

"Oooooh," Lisa cooed, becoming audibly moist.

She excused herself, presumably to mop up, and as she exited, Joey leaned over my shoulder. His hot breath on my neck felt strangely tantalizing.

"I know about you," he whispered.

Sweat began to form on my brow. Only Kurt knew the truth. I hadn't told another soul. What exactly did he know?

I had no choice, I decided, but to accept his abuse. There were no gay people at TravelNation, so being outed as a homosexual would result in not only complete social isolation, but likely dismissal. I felt for all the world like my teenage self, backed up against a locker.

● ● ●

"Eric, can you come down and see me?" Tess said as she passed by the bullpen.

Unlike Sheila, Tess did not terrify people, so I approached her office with far less fear for my personal well-being. Her back was turned to me as I entered.

"Thanks again for helping me get that column," I said brightly. "It sure is fun to do."

"Well, speaking of," she replied in an almost apologetic tone, "I showed a few of them to Jack."

This was incredibly flattering—her husband, Jack, was a superstar comedic personality on St. Louis morning radio. But judging from the tone of her voice, it had obviously not gone well. I steeled myself for his feedback. I was, after all, new at this, and advice or criticism from someone of his stature could only help make me better. If it didn't crush me.

She turned around and smiled mischievously. "He said if you want to send in some bits, he might do them on his show."

My jaw hit the ugly-industrial-carpeted floor. Jack thought I was good enough to write for *him*? Once again, someone seemed to be opening a door that I hadn't even thought to knock on.

I left her office fairly floating. I didn't have any particular dream of doing bits for a radio show, but maybe writing for someone as well-known as Jack could elevate my profile. Maybe this was a stepping-stone toward my dream of becoming the Boy Bombeck.

I wanted to run into the bullpen and shout the news. But this, I knew, would have to be under the radar. I didn't need to give Joey another reason to want to exact vengeance.

Then, one afternoon a few weeks later, as I walked into TravelNation, Lisa held up the latest newsletter.

"You've been writing stuff for Jack's radio show?!" she exclaimed, pointing to a news item on the second page. "Why didn't you tell us?"

"Oh!" I blurted out, horrified. I had no idea that Tess would blab. "It's nothing," I whispered, trying to shush her. "Just, like, jokey stuff."

"Stop being so modest. That's amazing!"

"Jack's just trying to help me out, that's all," I said quietly, sweat forming on my brow. "Let's not make a big thing out of it." I glanced down the hall to see Joey walking in the front door.

"Are you kidding?" she bellowed. "This is huge!"

Joey sauntered up to the group. He looked especially handsome today in his tightly fitted dress shirt. "What's huge?" He glanced at Lisa. "Besides your bazongas." He gave her a sexy smile and a thumbs-up. "Looking good."

"Eric," Lisa announced breathlessly, grabbing Joey's waist to draw him into the circle, "is writing stuff for Jack's radio show!" She put her other arm around me, so as not to betray her thrill at Joey's attention. "You're our very own star!"

I had been trying, for so many years, in so many arenas, to get someone to say these words. It was the culmination of years of searching and struggling and, all too often, failing. And it should have been thrilling. But in this moment, all I could picture was Joey announcing my queerness to the assembled crowd.

"Cool," Joey said insincerely. "What are they payin' ya?"

"Nothing," I replied. "It's just good experience."

"So, in other words, it's like that stuff you write here, huh?" he snorted. "You gotta do it for free to get anybody to use it?"

"Maybe right now," Lisa said. "But one day, he's gonna leave all of us behind."

"Well," Joey replied, "we know how much he likes behinds."

"Eric," Lisa said playfully, slapping my arm, "I didn't know you were an ass man."

• • •

The word quickly spread about my sideline with Jack's radio show. And as it did, something seemed to change.

People stopped coming up to me to suggest column ideas. They no longer seemed inclined to comment on jokes they particularly liked. These women who had long been so supportive of my creative endeavors changed the subject whenever I brought up my writing. It suddenly seemed as though the tide had turned, and people no longer wanted to hear about my dreams of becoming a real writer.

Had I become arrogant, I wondered? Was I focused too much on myself and not enough on others? Whatever the reason, the change in attitude from one of support and pride to one of determined indifference was striking.

One afternoon, as I rounded the corner to the break room to stash my Hungry Man dinner in the freezer, I heard several people talking. I stopped in my tracks.

"It's like, shut up, already. So you have a little talent," one of the women whispered.

"I know," another snapped, "you're not freaking George Carlin."

"I always thought he was such a nice guy," another said sotto voce, "until now."

I had always been someone who tended to put the needs of others ahead of my own—often to my own detriment. So it was painful to think that I was now viewed as someone who thought they were better than everyone else. Even if that bar was so low it could be used for a limbo contest.

A few minutes later, I cornered my friend Beth.

"Do people think I come off like a jerk?" I whispered.

"Well, you're just as dumb and pathetic as ever, as far as I'm concerned." She poked me in the ribs. "But that *is* kinda the word on the street."

"Why, what am I doing?"

She hesitated. "Well… Joey says all you do at night is brag about how you're gonna leave us all in the dust."

• • •

I knew that wasn't in my nature, but had I somehow behaved that way? Or was Joey just trying to get under my skin? I couldn't confront him about it, because having him turn on me would be even more disastrous. So I would have to turn this tide another way. I would, I decided, prove that I was self-deprecating. That I was aware of the needs of others. That, in Joey's case, I was all about him.

"Your hair looks great today," I said to Joey the next night as we sat working. "I wish," I added wistfully, "that I had hair like that."

"Thanks," he muttered.

"Mine has a mind of its own, and apparently, that mind is bat-shit crazy."

A couple of hours later, I turned to him. "Do you think this is really the beginning of a computer revolution, like they say?" I put my chin on my hand and gazed at him thoughtfully. "You'd know a lot better than I."

Lisa rolled her eyes.

The next night, just before Joey returned from dinner, I furtively unplugged my computer.

"Hey, can you help me?" I said plaintively as he walked in. "Something's wrong."

Joey sighed and crawled under the desk.

"God," I said with admiration as I stared at his Olympian physique sprawled out in front of me, "I wish I was good with computers like you are. That's a skill that's really useful."

An hour later, when Joey went to take a smoke break, Lisa pulled me aside.

"What are you doing?" she demanded. "This is weird."

"What are you talking about?" I said innocently.

"You have your head so far up his ass you could lick his tonsils."

"I do not!"

"Well, it sure looks that way. And you really need to knock it off. He's gonna think you're, like, in *love* with him or something. You want people thinking you're a fag?"

• • •

Although Joey seemed immune to my attempts to win his favor, my charm offensive seemed to be working, at least a bit, on the women in the office. As I made a point of avoiding any talk of my column or Jack and focused solely on their dating disasters and hormonal laments, the tide seemed to be turning a bit back into my favor.

One afternoon, Tess called me into her office again.

"Close the door."

I closed it and sat down.

"Jack and I were talking about you," she said matter-of-factly, referring to her celebrity husband. "We really think you're better than this job."

"I am?" I replied. "Tell that to Sheila. She walked into my room the other day wielding a letter opener. I think she was gonna stab me, but there were too many witnesses."

"Jack knows the creative director of an ad agency." She gazed at me. "Would you like him to get you an interview?"

Once again, a fork in the road of my new identity had presented itself.

"I can't make any promises," she added, "but what do you have to lose?"

I thanked her profusely and stumbled out, my head whirling. I had sold myself on the notion of a career as a columnist, not as an advertising person.

But this *was* a potential bird in the hand.

I slipped into the break room and sat down to think. The ad game definitely held a measure of glamour and prestige. I'd grown up worshipping *Bewitched*, and Darrin worked in an ad agency. I'd seen *Lover Come Back* with Rock Hudson and Doris Day on the old movie channel. And I'd written some commercials in a communications class at school—my professor had read one aloud as an example of "breakthrough" creative. So, maybe, if it was good enough for Darrin Stephens and Rock Hudson…

I imagined myself meeting with the heads of Fortune 500 companies.

I imagined myself drinking martinis at lunch and sleeping with my secretary.

I wondered if boys were ever secretaries.

• • •

I didn't breathe a word to anyone as I set to work.

Jack said that creative people needed "portfolios," so over the next several weeks, I spent all my free time writing sample scripts for commercials and public service announcements. I created radio spots for Six Flags and Mothers Against Drunk Driving on my cassette recorder, enlisting my friend Candace to sob into the microphone as a mom whose daughter has just been killed in a tragic car accident.

"Why, God," she shrieked, "why??!!"

"Okay, louder this time," I directed, "and not so whiny. I wanna feel bad for the mom, not wish she'd been in the car, too."

• • •

"*Who* are you, again?"

Merv Steinberg, a gruff, white-haired man in his fifties, stared up at me from behind a giant desk. He was the creative director of Steckler Advertising, and he didn't seem particularly glad to see me.

"Eric P-Poole," I stammered. "I was, uh, sent to you by Jack—"

"Oh, right," he said brusquely. He waved at the pleather portfolio case I was holding. I unzipped it and handed it to him.

There was silence for several minutes as he leafed through the materials. His face registered no sign of either approval or disgust.

He played the cassette. I searched his eyes for tears as car-crash sound effects blared from his tape deck and the sounds of Candace's tearful sobbing filled the room.

He switched it off.

"Yeah, okay. Thanks for coming in."

He handed me back the portfolio case. And it was over.

· · ·

As I walked into the lobby of TravelNation that afternoon, I was grateful that I had been wise enough not to tell anyone about the interview. As dejected as I was, at least I didn't have to explain my failure to everyone.

I glanced around. People were staring at me curiously.

"What?"

"Sheila wants to see you."

Had Tess told her about my interview? Surely she wouldn't do that to me. Maybe Lisa had blabbed about me writing my columns on company time. But what was the point of working unsupervised at night if we couldn't engage in a little white-collar crime?

I took a deep breath and knocked on Sheila's door.

"It's Eric."

"Come in."

I opened the door.

"Close it behind you." From the tone of her voice, this was not gonna be about a raise.

I carefully closed the door. As I turned to sit down in a chair, I saw a *Playgirl* magazine lying on her desk.

Well, that seems inappropriate, I thought. Unless she's in it. I'd always said that Sheila had the biggest balls in the office.

"Would you care," she said quietly, pointing to the magazine, "to explain this?"

I fumbled for an answer. "Well… you see, it's a dirty magazine for women."

"Would you care to explain," she said with a sigh, "why it was at your desk?"

My face went white.

"What? How did that…?" I was stunned. "That's not mine!"

"Eric, if this is something you're into," she said softly, "I make no judgments about it. It actually explains a lot of things." She leaned forward. "When I *care* is when you bring it in to work."

"I swear to you," I said, shaking, "I have never bought a magazine like that."

Not that I hadn't thought about it.

"Well, then, whose is it?"

"It must be some kind of joke," I said, breathing shallowly, my life flashing before my eyes. I hadn't gotten the advertising job, and now I was in danger of losing the job I *did* have.

She looked at me sternly. "You work at night. It's just you and Lisa and Joey. I know you think no one's around to see what you're up to, but—"

"I swear on my life," I said, getting mad now. "You have to believe me!"

She stared at me for a long moment.

"Well, if it isn't yours," she said, finally, "why would someone put it in there?"

"I have an idea," I replied grimly.

She threw the magazine into the trash and leaned back in her chair.

"Eric, I've never had anything but good feelings toward you. You've done a great job at this company." She fixed me with a steely look. "But this can never happen again, or it will be cause for immediate dismissal. My hands would be tied. Do you understand?"

"Yes, ma'am," I said quickly.

"Go."

I fled the office, steam coming out of my ears.

"Where's Joey?" I said to Lisa.

"I think he's in the conference room," she replied. "What happened in there?"

I turned without a word and marched down the hall. The conference room was a glassed-in affair, and as I approached it, I could see that he was alone. I threw open the door, walked in and slammed it behind me. Joey looked up from a speaker-phone he was working on.

"What?"

"Why are you doing this to me?"

"Doing what?" He continued to fiddle with the speaker-phone. I grabbed it away from him.

"Trying to make everyone think I'm gay, or something. That magazine," I said evenly. "It had to be you."

He looked at me blankly. "What magazine?"

"You're the only person who doesn't like me."

"Oh, yeah"—he snorted—"you're just beloved by everybody."

He stood up to leave, and I blocked the door.

"What did I ever do to you?"

"I think you're in love with me." He brushed by me. "And it grosses me out."

• • •

I didn't know what to do. I was almost positive it had been him, but I had no proof. Should I turn him in to Sheila? Should I quit? I didn't want to run away, but I didn't see how I could keep this up.

I fumbled through another workweek, avoiding Joey whenever possible, refusing to acknowledge him when it wasn't. He seemed unfazed by our confrontation, flirting with Lisa and soaking up the longing looks from various female employees with typical abandon.

Then, one afternoon in the second week following our confrontation, the mail arrived at home as I was preparing to leave for work. In it was a letter from Steckler Advertising.

I took a deep breath and tore it open. It was from Merv.

"I am pleased to offer you a position as junior copywriter," it began, "at a salary of $17,500 a year. Please call Susan in HR to discuss a start date and other employment details. We look forward to welcoming you to our company."

They were hiring me to write commercials. It wasn't my face on the cover of a book. But it was an affirmation that someone believed in me as a writer. Enough to pay me an offensively low salary.

Maybe I really *could* become the Boy Bombeck.

So nervous I could hardly speak, I called Steckler and set a start date in two weeks.

Mother and Dad were thrilled. Ever since I had abandoned my artistic dreams and gotten a "real" job, they had been delirious with delight.

"We know that creativity is important to you," Mother said. "But a paycheck's important to us."

"And come on," Dad added. "Writing jingles for cat food and stuff? You can't get much more creative than that."

• • •

When I arrived at TravelNation, I went straight to Sheila's office to tell her the news.

"I, um…" I fidgeted nervously, aware that this would not be considered good news. "I got a job in advertising. As a writer. I'm giving my notice."

She sighed heavily and frowned. Then, silently, she got up and walked around her desk. I instinctively flinched, moving back in my chair in case she wanted to leave a stiletto mark on my forehead as a parting gift.

She stood in front of me.

"I knew this day was coming."

And she put her arms out.

A bit shocked, I stood up, and Sheila Levine hugged me.

"I'm really proud of you."

We stood there for a long, slightly uncomfortable moment. She was so thin, I thought, as I felt her body against mine. I could snap her like a twig. She had always seemed so powerful, such a force of nature, and suddenly, she was just a woman.

A real person.

She pulled away and gazed into my face.

"If you don't like it there, just know—you can always come back." She smiled wistfully. "But I don't think you're gonna be coming back."

Word spread like wildfire.

Within an hour it seemed that the entire company knew, and I reveled in their excitement and pride.

"Wow," they marveled, "you're getting out of this hellhole."

"It's like you've been pardoned."

"What's it like," several people said, their eyes misty with longing, "to be free?"

I went to Tess's office and sat down in the chair in front of her desk.

"Thank you," I said awkwardly.

"For what?"

I kicked at an imaginary rock in the carpeting. "For, you know… believing in me."

"Aww, please," she said dismissively. "It was easy."

There was just one person left to tell.

An hour later, Lisa and I were sitting together at our desks when Joey walked in.

"Did you hear?" Lisa said excitedly.

"Hear what?" Joey said as he slipped off his jacket.

"Eric got a job at an ad agency."

He stopped in his tracks.

"He's gonna be a copywriter!" Lisa chirped.

I smiled up at him with a Cheshire cat grin. Joey fumbled with his keys and sunglasses, clearly off-kilter.

"Huh," he said softly. He cleared his throat. "Well, I guess if you can't stand the heat…"

"Oh, there's no heat," I said matter-of-factly as Lisa looked at us, confused at this seemingly coded conversation.

I crossed over to Joey's desk and leaned over. "There's no heat," I whispered in his ear, "'cause *you're not my type.*"

.... Chapter 10 ....

THAT BOY

"I'm here to see Donald."

I stood apprehensively in the foyer of a sophisticated high-rise apartment building in the rumored-to-be-gay section of the city called the Central West End. I say "rumored" because I had never set foot in this area before and had no idea what to expect, although I imagined hospitals with fashion-emergency rooms and daily church services to worship Sheena Easton.

Although it was 1984, this building reflected none of the bold color choices currently in vogue. It embraced a kind of hushed, old-world elegance that intimidated me and caused me to speak in a serious and professional tone, as if I were here for an organ donation instead of a blind date with someone I'd met in a cheesy personal ad.

Several weeks earlier, I had covertly placed an ad in the *Riverfront Times*, a city newspaper that actually had the

courage—or nerve, depending on your viewpoint—to offer
men-seeking-men and women-seeking-women ads in addi-
tion to the standard fare. Donald was the most promising of
the respondents, and we had corresponded back and forth via
a PO box I had covertly rented at our suburban post office,
since I knew that Mother and Dad weren't exactly up for reading mash notes from dudes.

Now that I had landed a job in advertising, my career was
finally beginning to take shape. So it was time, I decided, to
figure out exactly what this whole gay thing meant in my life.
I felt, I realized, like Ann Marie, Marlo Thomas's character
from the old sixties sitcom *That Girl*, who left her parents'
home to create a life for herself in the big city—and who had,
in the process, met a great guy named Donald Hollinger.

It *was* becoming a bit of a concern to me that many of
the people I found myself identifying with were women. But
women, it seemed, were the ones whose lives were changing
in this day and age. Women were the ones taking the steps to
forge new paths. And I'd come here today, I thought to myself,
to meet *my* Donald Hollinger.

The doorman of Donald's apartment building, an elderly,
uniform-clad gentleman, was perched behind a large polished
wood podium, where he spent what felt like several minutes
looking me up and down like I was a racehorse at Belmont.
He grunted disapprovingly. He shook his head. I wondered if
he would ask to see my teeth. He was stooped and wizened
and obviously offered no real security to the residents, but at
least he could sign for packages and judge your houseguests
with impressive condemnation.

"Donald who?"

I suddenly realized I had no idea what his last name was.

"That's funny," I laughed, a bit too loudly, leaning over his podium as if we were sharing an inside joke. "Donald... the *dentist*."

I smiled ingratiatingly. He didn't.

This was not how I wanted to start my new dating life. Weren't people supposed to be more liberal in the city? The last thing I needed was this creaky old bastard making me feel bad about who I was. I was good enough at that on my own.

Suddenly, I heard a voice from the elevator bank.

"Eric?"

I turned to find a cute, slightly goofy-looking guy striding toward me. This must be Donald, I thought, although he wasn't anything like he had described himself. About my age, he had curly blondish-brown hair and little round glasses and was wearing an expensive suit.

"I'm Rudy."

"I think you must be looking for another Eric...?" I said, confused.

"No, I'm a friend of Donald's. He's stuck on the phone upstairs and he sent me down to meet you."

Rudy led me over to some couches. "Pay no attention to the man behind the mahogany," he whispered, motioning dismissively to the doorman. "He's the same age as these sofas."

We began to chat. Immensely funny and likable, Rudy was an attorney at a prominent law firm, and I warmed to him immediately—especially once he revealed the actual reason he had been sent down on Donald's behalf.

"He's not on the phone," Rudy confided. "He just wanted me to make sure you weren't gross, or socially retarded, or a serial killer. So far, I'm pretty sure about the first two."

Rudy gave Donald the all-clear signal, and I stood nervously as the elevator door opened. A good-looking blond man, about six feet tall, walked into the lobby.

"This is Donald," Rudy said, introducing us. "Donald, this is Eric."

Although we were the same age, Donald was wearing a Ralph Lauren button-down shirt, perfectly shined penny loafers, and khaki pants. *This must be the uniform of the well-to-do*, I thought, making a mental note to see if I could find any of these items at Chess King. To my dismay, over this outfit he wore a waist-length mink jacket, which made him look exactly like a Long Island housewife.

"Nice to meet you," Donald said with a sort of teeth-baring sneer that revealed perfectly aligned teeth. He glanced at my Wham! T-shirt and jeans with what appeared to be a flash of disdain but I hoped was just a chill from the mink fresh out of storage.

"Hi," I replied brightly, "I'm surprised Rudy called you so soon—he still seemed kinda unsure about the serial killer thing."

"Yeah," Rudy said, turning to me, "you've got crazy eyes."

He said goodbye as Donald and I walked down the street to a trendy diner to have dinner. Although Donald was well put together, he wasn't exactly the embodiment of the Donald Hollinger of *That Girl*. Granted, I had little frame of reference for typical gay behavior. Maybe all homos wore fur and called their parents by their first names and used Estée Lauder Night Repair.

"I read somewhere," I said, attempting to make conversation as we walked, "that dentists have the highest rate of suicide of any profession except cops."

"Wouldn't you," Donald replied, "if you had to stick your hands in people's mouths all day? Between the bad breath and the kids who bite, I'm lucky if I don't gas myself to death before lunch." He sneered again, looking as if he'd just sniffed a turd, and this, I realized, was his version of a smile.

Donald took my hand as we entered the restaurant, a bold gesture that caused me to flinch momentarily. But no one seemed to bat an eye, and his nonchalance at this clearly queer act was sort of thrilling. As long as we didn't end up dead.

He whispered in my ear, "Enough about me. Let's talk about you."

His rather intimate behavior certainly indicated interest. And as dinner progressed, I began to reciprocate. This Donald wasn't a creative sort, like Ann Marie's boyfriend, who was a writer, but he *was* handsome. And he was from a wealthy patrician family who actually lived the kind of prestigious life I had always dreamed of for myself. And there was always the possibility, given the neighborhood, that someone would knock him down and steal the mink.

By the time we returned to his apartment—a sophisticated New York–style pied-à-terre, with hardwood floors and actual signed art on the walls—I had begun to imagine us as the perfect couple of *That Girl*.

Although that made me the girl.

• • •

Since Kurt had had the temerity to move to Ohio for his graduate studies, I called him regularly, often keeping him on the phone for hours as I plumbed the depths of his vast knowledge of the gay dating world. He had, after all, had nearly five dates over the past few years.

And I couldn't wait to wax poetic about Donald.

"Girl, is you trippin'?" Kurt interrupted before I had barely begun.

"Why?"

"You can't date mens and still live at home."

"Mens? Plural?"

"You'll give your parents a stroke. Word up."

"Stop talking like a teenage black girl."

"Sorry, I work with one. She's rubbing off on me. You gots to be movin' out, Miss Thing."

He was right. I was now lying to Mother and Dad constantly. And the biblical bomb throwing of B. R. Tibbits was taking its toll. Ann Marie had moved out on her own to forge a life for herself as a single woman in New York. Perhaps it was time to set myself free in St. Louis.

• • •

The first step would be the hardest. Although my sister, Val, had moved out years earlier, for some reason Mother and Dad seemed to regard their only son as a permanent and welcome fixture.

"Mother, Dad…" I said nervously over tuna casserole and my parents' new wine fancy, white zinfandel, "I think I'm gonna move out."

Dad's face went white. Mother dropped her fork. "No!" she shrieked before she could stop herself.

"What would you wanna do *that* for?" Dad said.

"Uh, people are starting to think I'm under house arrest."

"That's crazy. Your life's barely begun!"

"And that's the problem. It can't really begin until I live on my own."

"Lots of kids live at home until they get married, you know," Mother said. "Your sister did."

"Well," I said timidly, "I don't have any plans to get married."

Mother unconsciously grabbed Dad's hand. "Of course not," she said, her voice strangely tremulous. "You're just... focused on your job. That's good."

"It's responsible," Dad added quickly.

"I hope you realize, though," Mother said, gripping her wine glass so tightly that her knuckles were turning white, "that building a career takes a lot of energy. You probably shouldn't plan on having any social outings."

"That's right," Dad added. "None. Really, none at all." He paused. "Well, except maybe when Kurt comes home to visit. He sounds like a nice boy."

• • •

The next order of business was to determine where I wanted to reside. Obviously, in order to live an openly gay life that Mother and Dad wouldn't get wind of, I would need to create a buffer zone. I decided to move into the city, which was becoming slightly less dangerous than in years past but which still, in the minds of St. Louis suburbanites, required friendship with a pimp and proximity to a SWAT team.

This would also put me in Donald's vicinity, which would make our blossoming relationship less cumbersome. But in order to live in an apartment that Donald would agree to visit, I would need to find something stylish.

Although I loved my new advertising job, my salary at Steckler basically afforded me Chiclets and deodorant, so getting a roommate was essential. I quickly (some might argue too quickly) settled on an acquaintance named Carl, a blond, dynamic RN who had tried to seduce me in his nursing school dorm room when we first met.

Once we got past this awkward moment, we discovered that we had a lot in common, most notably the desire to get the hell out of the house. We began shopping for an apartment and settled on one in DeBaliviere Place, a newly rehabbed neighborhood not far from Donald's, where the developer had retained the turn-of-the-century building facades but gutted the classic interiors. The apartment we selected, in a beautiful brick six-plex, was large and airy and completely devoid of either character or insulation. But it was ours.

As I prepared for the move, I began to fantasize about my big new *That Girl* life: Carl and me sharing a party bag of Funyuns and watching *Fame* on our nineteen-inch Zenith TV; performing routines from *Flashdance* in the living room; mixing up freeway frosties (liquor libations in to-go cups) before heading out to the bars together for a night of earsplitting fraternal bonding.

My vision continued with images of Donald and me enjoying tête-à-têtes at trendy boîtes where the owners comped our meals because our presence was such a draw, and celebrating birthdays with our massive group of friends, which now included the St. Louis hoi polloi like gossip columnist Jerry Berger, who knew Ethel Merman personally.

I had taken the first step toward a new life. I was ready to become That Boy.

• • •

By 6:00 p.m. on the day of our move, Carl and I were excitedly settling into our new apartment. The joie de vivre was palpable. I had finished hanging the pictures, all my boxes had been unpacked and removed, and I was celebrating my newfound freedom by scrubbing the bathtub when Carl walked in.

"Wow," he whistled, looking around at my neatly arranged bedroom. "I haven't even set up my bed. We may need to use yours later."

I looked up from a cloud of Comet. "We?"

"I've got a friend coming over."

"Tonight? But it's our first night. I thought we'd just kind of get settled…?"

"No worries, I told him he can't stay long. I wanna make it out to the bars by eleven."

In concert with Carl's attempt to nail me the day we met, some might consider this information a clue, indicating a pattern of perhaps questionable behavior. But in my desperation to begin a new life, I elected to regard it as a whimsical quirk. Perhaps, in retrospect, I should have taken his joke about installing a drive-through lane in his bedroom at face value, but I assumed he just meant he liked to eat fast food under the covers.

"Oh, you're going out tonight?" I said. "Maybe I can go with you."

This outing, I thought, could be the true initiation of our friendship, a night we would long look back upon with affection and fondness.

"No, thanks," he replied. "I work alone."

• • •

Initially, I loved the sense of freedom I was experiencing. Here, twenty-five miles away from home, I could cram the cupboard full of Suzy Qs. I could leave water in the kitchen sink, willy-nilly. I could get drunk and cook Tater Tots in the nude (not recommended, I discovered, since passing out with them still in the oven results in a lecture from unreasonably irritated firemen). I could be myself.

Unfortunately, I was mostly *by* myself. I had envisioned living with someone as popular as Carl as a springboard to a new, exciting world, but it was quickly becoming a new and lonely world. Carl was incredibly adept at making friends—most of whom appeared to be made in his bedroom and which involved a high-decibel exchange of proclamations that no level of TV sound could ameliorate—but he preferred to keep them to himself.

These new friends, on the other hand, preferred to keep my personal *property* to themselves. I would frequently find one of them crouching over my TV or stereo, calculating its weight and the dimensions of our front door with a disconcerting level of interest. Eventually, when I confronted Carl about the Villeroy & Boch ashtray and my brand-new Swatch watch that had gone missing, he was remorseful.

"If I remembered their names," he said cheerfully, jabbing his elbow into my ribs, "I'd try to get that stuff back."

Unfortunately, his idea of reparations involved invitations that were inevitably postponed due to his irresistibility to others.

"Hey, can we do dinner another night?" he would say as he slipped into a pair of jeans so tight you could actually hear the screams of the seams. "I met this superhot guy at the free clinic."

At least I had Donald. Although he didn't seem to want us to spend a lot of time alone together, he thoroughly enjoyed our dates out on the town. And on a certain level, I understood. AIDS was everywhere in the news, and we were both determined not to catch this awful disease. It was really best if we kept our relationship a chaste one.

"Where would you like to go to dinner?" I queried one night, ever conscious of my meager entertainment budget. "If you don't mind the early-bird special, we could go to Silk Road."

"Eric," Donald said with a condescending half sneer, "I don't eat food that is on *sale*."

He saw the hurt look on my face and began to backpedal. "Why don't we go to Balaban's," he offered, which I knew was his favorite restaurant, an expensive society café. "My treat."

Dinner—at a candlelit table next to the large wood-framed windows that opened onto the street, was romantic and sophisticated. Even if half the words on the menu—vichyssoise, mussels meunière—were a complete mystery.

"Wow," I said as I surveyed the menu, "it changes *every day*? Maybe that's why they don't laminate it."

"If it's the last thing I do," Donald replied, "I will cure you of eating chili dogs at Der Wienerschnitzel."

Donald knew everyone, and given that we'd only been dating a month, he seemed to relish introducing me to the movers and shakers who came up to the table.

"This is Eric," he said, grabbing my hand when someone approached. "We're *lovers*."

I was alternately taken aback at this statement (particularly since, given our fears about disease transmission, we had done very little) and glad that I had moussed my hair for the occasion.

After the third time, I leaned over to him.

"Can I tell you something?"

"Sure," he replied.

"I don't really like that word."

"What word?"

"Lovers."

"Why?"

"I don't know. I guess it just sorta conjures up images people don't really need right before the soup comes."

"Oh, relax."

"Besides, it's not true."

"Well, maybe it will be." He smile-sneered.

Was this, I wondered, his way of saying that tonight would be the night that we express our feelings in some sort of safe yet acrobatic manner? And what were my feelings? Donald was dry and awfully pretentious, and I wasn't entirely sure that he was for me, but he was cute enough. And I was lonely enough.

• • •

As we crossed through the lobby of Donald's apartment building, I covertly popped a piece of Dentyne into my mouth while Donald nodded at Horace, who grunted disapprovingly.

As the elevator doors closed, I took a deep breath and made my move. Pushing Donald up against the wall with what I felt was a sexy, That Boy swagger, I breathed hotly into his ear.

"I guess I owe you something," I said huskily, "for dinner."

He wriggled out of my grasp. "Umm," he said nervously, "there's something I think I should tell you."

I backed away and gazed at his face, searching for a sign. He looked sheepish.

"I really want to do it," he said softly. "You're adorable, and I like you. But… well…" He paused. "I'm just not ready."

He kissed me and stepped off the elevator.

"He's a man of honor," I said to Kurt on the phone the next night. "When the time comes, he wants it to be right."

"You be trippin', Sister Sledge."

"You're doing it again."

"Sorry. But telling people that you're lovers and then not wanting to do anything? No diggity, *gurl*, that boy's Le Freak."

• • •

For months now, I had postponed going home to visit Mother and Dad, hesitant as I was to revisit the scene of the crime. Finally, after repeated phone pleas and cards with sentiments like "We hope you're not dead," I offered a compromise and invited them to dinner at the apartment.

"You're gonna need to de-gay the house."

This from Carl, who was apparently unaware that he would be item number one on that list. Although he was quite masculine and could easily "pass," his tendency to blurt out statements like, "I'd like to hunt that Michael J. Fox!" or greet someone with, "Hey, you big fag!" could be somewhat problematic.

I evaluated our decor. Given that Mother had been buying me Waterford stemware for several years, I wasn't entirely sure what to remove. Maybe the *Dreamgirls* poster. And the Lucite "Please Take One" dispenser that Carl had nailed up in the hallway leading to his bedroom, which was filled with condoms.

The appointed evening of their visit, Carl thoughtfully left just as I was sliding the aluminum pan of toasted ravioli into the oven. As luck would have it, the idea of spending the evening pretending that the nursing profession was rife with men who reproduced didn't exactly set his world aflame.

As I scoured the premises for questionable items like Culture Club albums and Sea & Ski self-tanner, Dad called.

"Hey, which car do you think is less likely to have its hubcaps stolen?"

I sighed. He and Mother obviously envisioned having to fight off crack whores as they entered the building.

"You'll be fine," I replied. "Leave the brass knuckles at home."

About forty minutes later, I glanced out the window to see them running toward the building as if dodging grenades.

"Didn't you know," I said calmly as I opened the front door, "that we're in the DMZ?"

"We were just in a hurry to get here," Dad said, knowing even before he finished this statement that no one bought it.

"What a beautiful neighborhood," Mother exclaimed. "Such lovely old buildings."

"Yeah," Dad added. "It's like some of the ones we blew up during the war."

Mother handed me a shopping bag from Dillard's.

"A little housewarming gift. We weren't sure what you needed."

I opened the bag to find an Aromatique Summer Sorbet–scented candle. Mother loved shopping for Val and me; at any given time, the basement of their house was so stocked with gifts that it could serve as a Macy's fulfillment center.

"Thank you!" I enthused. "This will really cover the smell of the rats and the burning trash."

As I began to show them around the apartment, they seemed somewhat reticent, as if hesitant to leave the "public" areas, spending considerable time oohing and aahing over the ugly sofa Val had generously given me.

"You've seen that before, you know," I said, mystified at their enthusiasm. "It's from her basement. Come see my bedroom."

Eventually, I pried them away and they stepped uneasily into the bedroom, stopping just past the threshold.

"Where's Carl?" Dad asked. He seemed nervous.

"Oh, he had an emergency," I replied. "Saving lives is a 24-7 job." I had told Mother and Dad that Carl was a doctor, since nursing smacked of girliness.

"And where's *his* bedroom?"

"It's on the other side of the apartment, off the dining room."

"Oh, how nice!" Mother enthused. "He has his own room!" They turned and made a beeline for it.

Fortunately, for a slut, Carl was very neat, and all items of a personal nature were safely tucked away, so his bedroom was quite presentable, outside of the airplane hangar–size box fan he required for white noise, which could be heard several blocks over.

"Look at that," Mother whispered to Dad, as they swept into Carl's room. "His own bed and everything."

Surely, I thought, the color draining from my face, they didn't think…?

I quickly popped open the spigot on a brand-new box of Franzia and we sat down to dinner.

"Well, you boys have a lovely apartment," Mother said. "Are you glad you made the move?"

Not really, I thought to myself. *The grass definitely isn't greener.*

"Well, sure!" I said, mustering as much enthusiasm as possible, unwilling to admit defeat. "Are you kidding? It was the best thing I ever did!"

For a brief moment, Mother and Dad looked as if I'd hit them in the face with a two-by-four.

"Oh," Mother said softly. "I guess we didn't know you'd been so unhappy."

I wanted to crawl into a hole. "I wasn't really unhappy," I quickly backpedaled. "I just meant…"

"That's okay," Dad said. "We knew you had to leave sometime. We just hoped it would be when you were forty."

"Really. I wasn't unhappy."

Mother and Dad both nodded understandingly, but I felt as if I had negated an entire lifetime of child rearing in one stupid statement. A statement I hadn't even meant.

The room grew quiet. I took a large gulp of wine.

"Actually," I said, "I'm unhappy now."

"Oh," Mother said, "why is that?"

"I don't know," I said. "Carl and I aren't really friends, and… it's just a little lonely."

"Well, you can come have dinner with us any time you want," Dad said. "There's always plenty of Spam."

"Thanks."

"You know what?" Mother tapped her wine glass to signal Dad to tilt the box in her direction. "These people don't know what they're missing."

"That's for sure," Dad added. "There aren't many like you out there."

"Anybody who doesn't understand how terrific you are," Mother said, "doesn't deserve you."

I felt a little bit like crying. I hadn't realized how much I had looked forward to being with two people who looked forward to being with me.

"These toasted ravioli are delicious," Dad said, almost chipping a tooth on one. "How'd you get them so crispy?"

"I burned 'em."

• • •

When Mother and Dad left, I decided that the one thing that could cap this lovely night would be to share it with the person I was dating. Even if that person was Donald.

When I arrived at his apartment building, Rudy was walking out the front door.

"Hey!" I said brightly, happy to see him. "Nice to see you again."

"You, too," he said, a bit nervously. "Are you here to see…?"

"Yeah, thought I'd just surprise him."

"Uhhh," he said awkwardly, "I don't think I'd do that."

"I know," I said, chuckling, "he's not the most spontaneous person, but—"

"No, really," Rudy said, grabbing my arm. "Don't go up there."

"Why?"

He dragged me over to a couch in the lobby and sat me down.

"Listen," he said furtively, as if the cops were on his tail. "I didn't tell you this…"

"Tell me what?" I said, mystified.

"Donald's up there with his ex."

"What ex?" I said, dumbstruck. "He has an *ex*?"

"Yeah. Trust me, they'll be back together any day now. It'd take two accountants, three attorneys, and six therapists to separate those idiots. They've dated for two years. They've only been broken up for two months."

I could feel the heat rising in my face.

Sorry," Rudy said apologetically. "Please don't shoot the messenger, but *somebody* should tell you the truth. It's been killing me to keep this secret."

"So, he was never really interested in me?"

"No. He just wanted to make Robert jealous."

I felt the rug of my *That Boy* empowerment being summarily yanked out from under me.

"I'm gonna go up there," I said, gritting my teeth.

"You can't," Rudy replied. "Horace has to key the elevator for you, and Donald will tell him not to."

"I wanna catch him in the act!"

"Don't make this a *Dynasty* moment," Rudy said. "You don't have the shoulder pads for it."

I stared down at the floor, humiliated.

"Trust me, you're better off," Rudy said. "You're not exactly a troll who lives under a bridge, you know."

"Thanks," I said, feeling for all the world like a troll who lives under a bridge.

Rudy cocked his head.

"Hey, tell you what," he said. "I was just heading out to meet some friends at Nights. You wanna come?"

Nights was a tacky gay nightclub that played dance music at rafter-shaking levels and, more importantly, had no cover. A hodgepodge of vaguely country-western and disco elements, with a sunken dance floor and stroke-inducing lights, the bar was frequented by students and priests from the local Catholic universities.

By the time I was on drink number two, Rudy and I were on the dance floor, working up a sweat to the Pointer Sisters' "Jump." As I did an innovative kick step that I had worked out in front of the mirror at home, I noticed a tall, pretty brunette girl smiling at me.

"Nice move!" she yelled over the music.

"Thanks!" I hollered back. "It's patent pending."

I kept catching her eye as we danced and found myself somewhat awed by her sense of ease in this setting. She seemed to be a straight girl, but she was totally cool with the environment. I wanted to be friends with a girl like this— someone who not only didn't mind that I was gay, but who would dance to Bananarama.

It was time to be That Boy.

When the song ended, I followed her off the dance floor.

"I'm Eric," I said, sticking my hand out.

"Diane," she replied, shaking it. She gazed at me for a moment. "You look familiar. Did I see you at a travel show a while back?"

"Maybe," I replied. "I used to be a travel agent. So, you're in travel?"

"I work for a tour company," she replied, pushing her shoulder-length hair back with one hand. "Taking care of cranky tourists on seven-day bus tours."

"So, that's why you need a drink."

"You have no idea. I'd mainline heroin, but those bus rides are bumpy."

I chuckled. "So, what are you doing *here*?"

She pointed across the bar to a good-looking blond guy who was chatting up another man.

"I'm his fag hag," she replied. "The pay sucks, but I get to meet nice guys I can never have."

By the time she and Rudy and I ended up at a diner at midnight, I was charmed. And somewhat heartened. For although my first relationship had just ended in a fiery car crash of humiliation, I seemed to have made two new friends.

At 1:00 a.m., Rudy begged off, leaving Diane and me alone at the diner.

"How come Scott didn't leave with you?" I asked, referring to Diane's friend at the bar.

"Oh, I always drive separately," she replied. "It's bad enough I have to see all these guys he drags back to our apartment. I don't need to watch them play grab-ass in the car."

She gazed at me. "So, you're sure you're gay, huh?"

"Pretty much," I replied, smiling.

"Damn. How come you're single? You seem like a catch."

"Tell that to Donald Parker."

"Donald Parker...?" she said thoughtfully. "Does he wear a fur?"

"That's the guy."

"Why," Diane said as she munched on a French fry, "why would you wanna date somebody who clutches the lapels of his coat like he's modeling for Dicker and Dicker of Beverly Hills?"

I laughed heartily. I liked this lanky, funny girl. She barely knew me and already seemed to care more about me than Donald ever had. I wished I could marry *her*, I thought as I gazed at her wide-set eyes and warm, open smile. I wondered how much liquor that would require.

"So," I said, changing the subject, "you and Scott live together?"

"Yeah," she replied. "And the only bathroom in our apartment is inside my bedroom. I have half-naked guys wandering past my bed at all hours."

"I know what you mean about the endless parade of tricks," I said. "My roommate, Carl, doesn't even seem to have a type. Every morning, it's like breakfast at the United Nations."

"How did we end up with these idiots?" Diane said.

"More importantly," I replied, "how do we get rid of them?"

• • •

A few weeks later, "It's Raining Men" was blasting from Carl's bedroom as I knocked on the door.

"Come in!" he hollered.

Given that he was never one for modesty, I was unsurprised to find him runway modeling some new underwear that was roughly the size of a Post-it note and dental floss.

"Carl," I began loudly, "I, uh, need to talk to you about something…"

"I'm all ears!" he replied, as if those were the only things uncovered.

Carl loved our living situation. I knew he wasn't going to take this well. I took a deep breath.

"You're a great guy," I yelled hesitantly, averting my eyes for multiple reasons, "and a good roommate. I mean, other than your dates stealing stuff, and you not always paying your bills on time, and you—"

"I gather that compliment's under construction?"

"Sorry," I said apologetically. "I guess I'm a little nervous. This isn't easy."

"Good thing I am!" he replied merrily, as if he'd actually come up with this line.

"You should travel with your own rimshot," I replied, as if I'd actually come up with that one. "See, I have this friend,

Diane, and she's in a bad living situation. She really needs to get out of it, and I really want to help her, and I was thinking… maybe she and I should live together."

I winced. Would he react with hurt or anger? Would he beg me to stay, or tell me off? I suspected this would devastate him, for although Carl had many "friends," he didn't have many friends.

"Can she move in on the first?" he said as he bent over to road test the floss. "Kamal and I are a couple now"—I had no idea which headboard banger he was referring to—"and he's been begging me to move in with him, so I finally said yes."

• • •

"What do you wanna do tonight?" I asked Diane, as we dined on Chicken McNuggets by candlelight. We'd been roommates now for two blissful months.

"Let's go to Nights," she replied. "It's All You Can Drink Tuesday. If we get there early enough, we can have six drinks for five bucks. That's eighty-three cents a screwdriver."

An hour later, as we stepped into the eardrum-blowing ambience of Nights, I heard a voice.

"So you're the guy who stole my roommate."

I turned around to see Scott, Diane's sexy former roommate.

"I'm just borrowing her," I said, smiling. "You can have her back when she's too old to be a man magnet."

Diane slugged me.

"I think," Scott said suggestively, "that it was *your* force field that attracted me."

And as he flirted with me, and I sneaked a knowing smile

at Diane, I realized that, with just a little boldness, I had turned my life around. I had a roommate who enjoyed my company and appreciated a bargain. And I had a new life in the big city.

I had become That Boy.

·· Chapter 11 ····

WHO CAN TURN THE WORLD ON WITH HIS WIG

"Why do you think he's gonna fire me?"

I was on my second drink and fueled with rotgut terror. As I sat at the local dive bar with my coworkers from the advertising agency where I now worked, I held a panicked conference with my boss, Kristina.

"I can just tell," she whispered as she cleaned the lenses of her glasses, which were slightly larger than the circumference of her face. "He told me he thinks you're dull."

I had been called many things in my life. Fairy. Fem. Clownfucker. (Don't ask.) But none stung quite as much as "dull"—especially coming from Kristina, a cheery Keebler elf who doubled as the agency's associate creative director. She was brilliantly talented and from day one had been my champion.

"I *know* you're creative, but you gotta speak up, say your ideas out loud." She motioned to the seventies Blaxploitation hairdo I was currently sporting due to the humidity. "There's bound to be some great ideas under that bad haircut."

I had always loved Mary Tyler Moore. Her seminal TV show had been a huge part of my formative years, and I had closely identified with her character, Mary Richards: that eagerness to please, the distaste for confrontation, and, as the years progressed, Mary's growing sense that she had value in the world.

And now, as I tried to establish a foothold at my first "career" job—as a junior copywriter at Steckler Advertising—I realized how much my path was mirroring Mary's: I lacked confidence. I felt out of place. And I had a cranky, obstreperous boss.

As a copywriter, I was expected to come up with fresh and innovative ideas for print ads, radio spots, and TV campaigns. But having only written humor columns, I had no real clue how this was done. And three months into the job, Greg, the president of the agency, was losing patience.

Soon, I thought, *I'll be crawling back to the travel agency, tail between my legs. Joey will probably wet himself with glee.*

"So…" I whispered to Kristina, "how long do I have?"

"I don't know, a few weeks?" she replied. "I think he's already putting out feelers for new writers, but it'll take him a while to find somebody who'll work for—"

"Indentured servitude?"

"Yeah."

"Less money than a barefoot girl in a Chinese sweatshop?"

"See, this is what I'm talking about. Why can't you be like this in a meeting?"

As I pondered the fear that held me back, my eyes settled

on the Wall, a large, illustrated listing of nine wildly differ-ent cocktails on one wall of the bar, which, if successfully consumed, were comped. The commemorative photos of the brave, vomit-flecked, cross-eyed few who had accomplished this feat were displayed, appropriately enough, in the hallway leading to the toilets.

"I'm not sure why," I replied. "Maybe the Wall will provide some answers."

• • •

One week passed at Steckler, and although many oppor-tunities arose for me to offer up ideas, I remained mum. I wondered if this would be where my path diverged from that of Mary Richards. Although I had Mary's sense of style, and her desire to make her mark in the world, my Lou Grant didn't seem to secretly have a soft spot for me.

I took to dodging Greg. Since this was particularly tricky in the bathroom, I began ducking into the women's room and peeing sitting down, until a pushy account executive stuck her hand under the stall and asked to borrow a tampon.

Kristina took me aside. "We all pitch ideas," she said patiently, "and most of 'em totally suck. But sometimes you've gotta say something really stupid to get to something really good. And I know you can say something stupid. I've seen you drunk."

Another week passed. Time and again I attempted to sum-mon my courage but was stopped in my tracks by the notion that there were degrees to stupid ideas, and what if the stupid thing I offered up was totally, unequivocally dreadful?

The drumbeat of failure began to pound in my head as I

contemplated the possibility of having to return to TravelNation, of hugely disappointing my mother, who—in quarterly newsletters designed to engender resentment and self-loathing in friends and relatives—had told everyone that I was now an "advertising professional managing an impressive list of regional blue-chip clients."

Why couldn't I just say one idea out loud?

Week three, Kristina began to withdraw, obviously sensing the inevitability of my dishonorable discharge. Every day that passed became more painful, as my conscience screamed in my good ear, "Speak up!"

On Friday, as we sat in her office discussing a radio script for the Famous-Barr department stores, the door flew open as if someone was blowing a bank vault. Greg charged in.

This wasn't unusual behavior. A handsome, macho, large-framed man in his early forties, Greg was a tornado of ambition and bravado. And as a practicing Catholic, he knew the kinds of things that got confessed behind closed doors.

And now, here he stood, the executioner of my dreams. I closed my eyes, awaiting my sentence, hoping death would come quickly, bloodlessly.

"Jack's retiring," he barked at Kristina, referring to the agency's CEO. "We need a going-away video. Party's in two weeks." He roared off down the hall.

I opened my eyes, stunned by the absence of words like *fired* and *loser* and *dead to me*. Had I had been reprieved, at least for now?

That night, Kristina and I and several other creative department folk rendezvoused at the bar to brainstorm ideas for the video. Kristina, my mentor and cheerleader, all but ignored me, and I wanted to be anywhere but there. I immediately downed drink number one on the Wall, a Singapore Sling, hoping to dull the nervous thrumming that kept my brain in tilt mode.

Nearly an hour passed, and slowly, my body relaxed as the warmth of drink number two began to render me comatose. About the time we started on drink number three, Riley, a bubbly, freckle-faced brunette who was attempting to get her photo tacked up by the toilets, came up with the idea of using the old Ray Charles song "Hit the Road, Jack" as the theme to the video. Now half in the bag, my mental defenses only fitfully standing guard, I suddenly spoke without thinking.

"How about if we had a girl group called Riley and the Rilettes?"

Everyone turned to look at me, startled. The slur in my grain-fermented voice only added to what was obviously a preposterous idea. There was a pause, and I put my head down, horrified at what I had just done. I was afraid to look at anyone. I wanted to crawl into my drink and drown.

"That is high-*larious*!" Kristina hollered, slapping me on the arm, her eyes sparkling, an expression of motherly pride spreading across her face. "In fact, I think we should have costumes made!"

Everyone began to build on the idea as my face flushed with delight and cheap liquor. It felt as though I had been knighted.

Riley and Emma, a beautiful preppy-turned-punk goddess, quickly signed on as Riley and a Rilette. Kristina polled the group for more volunteers.

"Come on, who else? We need at least one more."

The warm glow I felt began to chill when Simon, another writer (who bought pot by the pound and whom we affectionately referred to as the Weed Whacker), suddenly snapped out of his reefer madness.

"Let's make Eric the other Rilette!"

• • •

Proving the old adage that no good deed goes unpunished, the notion of me in drag was roundly applauded, and within days of my stupid moment of boldness, Rilettes costumes were covertly assembled: poodle skirts, yellow-and-black bowling shirts with our names embroidered on them, nylons, bobby socks, and red high-heeled pumps.

At eight one night, when most of the employees had gone home, Riley, Emma, and I assembled in the women's bathroom. There, they accessorized my Rilette look with enough lipstick, eye shadow, and rouge to fell a drag queen, courtesy of the fishing tackle box of makeup that resided on the desk of the agency's receptionist, who moonlighted as a cheerleader for the St. Louis Cardinals. (She could typically be found rehearsing slutty dance routines in the lobby, to the inexhaustible annoyance of the company's female executives and the infinite delight of Greg, the president.)

They both stood back, oohing and aahing at their own handiwork. I felt like a Picasso painting and, indeed, closely resembled one.

"You," Riley declared, "are a *glamazon.*"

"Don't hate me because I'm beautiful," I replied.

"Somewhere, right now," Emma added, "Grace Jones is nervous."

They pushed me out the door and stood watching as I wobbled down the hall. The only other time I had actually worn women's clothing was when, at age ten, I had tried on one of Mother's pantsuits and some bangle bracelets in an unconscious ode to Florence Henderson.

As I passed the Weed Whacker, he whistled appreciatively. "I'd do ya!"

Oddly, I was beginning to enjoy the attention. Or I was beginning to enjoy being someone else. I knew a little something about that.

Laurel, an account executive, rounded the corner and shrieked involuntarily.

"Oh my God, your boobs look so real!"

She high-fived me.

It seemed peculiar that this would be her first reaction to seeing me in drag, but given that she had recently gotten implants and her breasts now looked like two watermelons superglued to her collarbone, perhaps her focus was somewhat singular.

I clomped into Kristina's office. She gasped. "Wow. You're so…"

"Scary?" I replied. "Whorish? Troubled?"

"Different," she said admiringly. "My little Eric's been replaced by…"

"A seven-foot transvestite with a smattering of adult acne."

"I know this is kind of embarrassing, but listen, if Greg doesn't think you're a keeper after this…"

"Then everyone will speak of the tragic moment when a young copywriter destroyed his career. A myth will emerge. I'll be a legend." I tugged at my bobby socks. "I'll also be unemployed."

Riley, Emma, and Simon all entered.

"Okay," Kristina said, clapping her hands. "Let's get this show on the road. Who's choreographing?"

We all looked at each other.

"I guess I could…" I said tentatively. "Why don't we start in the women's john?" I knew it so well now. "We could each jump out of a stall in time to the intro."

• • •

The video was a smash. Dozens of coworkers complimented my creativity, my bravery, and my booty. This wasn't exactly how I'd hoped to achieve it, I thought to myself, but maybe I *could* take a nothing day and suddenly make it all seem worthwhile.

Greg, however, remained an enigma.

"Did he like it?" I asked Kristina the following Monday.

"Yeah, I think he felt you exhibited a lot of creativity." She sighed. "The problem is, he also thought you exhibited homosexual tendencies."

As if waiting for his cue, the door suddenly blew off its hinges and Greg barged in.

"Nice job on the video," he said, to no one in particular. Then, he turned casually to me. "Too bad your girlfriend couldn't be there to see it."

"What girlfr—?" I started to say, then immediately froze with fear as I realized what was happening.

I had never discussed, with Kristina or anyone else at the agency, the fact that I was gay. While I had indeed begun to live more openly, there were, in my mind, clear and concrete limits—and those limits included not revealing my true nature to my very Catholic boss. This job had given me an identity, a focus, a chance at a life that offered at least some measure of excitement and creative fulfillment. And I couldn't risk throwing that all away.

"Uh," I replied, "I don't think she could have made it all the way from Kansas City."

Kansas City was the first place that sprang to mind, given that I had spent my entire childhood visiting my extended family there. I marveled at my quick thinking, since a long-distance relationship would require less documentation.

"What's her name?" Greg demanded.

"Kitty." From Kansas City. At this point, rhyming it for easy recall just seemed practical.

There was a long pause.

"Kitty, huh?"

"Yep… Kitty."

Kristina shifted uncomfortably in her seat.

"Well," Greg said, chuckling, a snarky grin on his face, "you tell Kitty that I said you are one *ugly* woman." He spun around and blew down the hall.

• • •

Other people at the ad agency seemed to be developing a bit of respect for me, but I felt no closer to earning Greg's approval than I had been on day one.

One afternoon a few days later, he waltzed into my "office," a videotape storage room into which a children's desk had been wedged. This was no mean feat, since the room was so tight that entering or exiting required lube and a diet plan.

"McDonald's is starting a new campaign called Mac

Tonight," he barked. "I need somebody to visit the local restaurants as the Mac character. It pays seventy-five bucks a pop. Nobody wants to do it."

Could this be my moment, I wondered, my opportunity to win him over once and for all?

I momentarily fantasized becoming a hit as Mac Tonight, and Greg clasping my hand warmly in appreciation, inviting me over for drinks at his glamorous Ladue home with him and the missus, where he would confide his long-held belief in me and tell me how he had carefully mapped out his campaign of "tough love."

"I'll do it!" I yelped, relieved that this exercise in creativity did not involve a beehive hairdo or lip gloss.

I was, however, unaware that the character in question was actually a *costume* character like those found at Disneyland, but without the perks of customer familiarity, bathroom breaks, or free funnel cake.

The costume was a thirty-six-inch-high heavy plastic half-moon head with Ray-Bans, which sat on my shoulders. Unfortunately, no one had done the math on this and realized that a roughly eight-foot-tall dancing moon man might be disturbing to certain younger patrons.

I began to realize that this might not be quite the resounding success I envisioned when my roommate Diane and I made our first appearance at a South County McDonald's. Diane was joining me on these personal appearances to serve as boom-box wrangler, and as we entered, she threw the door open and loudly proclaimed, "Ladies and gentlemen… Mac Tonight!"

She switched on a cassette tape, which began to blare a jazzy, distorted version of the old Bobby Darin song "Mack the Knife" with McDonald's-themed lyrics. I performed a Fosse-esque swing step through the doorway without accounting for the height of my head and was immediately knocked to the ground.

Many older kids laughed and pointed, as toddlers shrieked in fear and parents held them close, unsure if I was about to pull out free coupons or a gun. Since the television campaign hadn't been running terribly long, clearly most people had no idea who the hell I was supposed to be.

"Oh my God!" Diane whispered. She knelt down and helped me up, and, a little dizzy, I began to dance around the restaurant, attempting to charm families with my sophisticated Mac Tonight persona. Greg had reassured me that children would be dazzled by this unique character, but, outside the accepted realm of a theme park, most seemed to regard it as an opportunity—indeed, a personal challenge—to bully someone who couldn't fight back. Images of TravelNation and childhood torture came flooding back as I attempted to keep my anger and the surprisingly real prospect of suffocation at bay.

Diane's role quickly devolved from boom-box wrangler to riot police. By the time she had smacked a twelve-year-old who was throwing fries at my head and screamed, "I'll wipe that grin right off your face, you little freak!" we were ushered from the building.

Subsequent appearances didn't fare much better, but Diane and I finally made peace with the taunts by taking periodic breaks out back by the restaurant dumpsters, where, to the trauma of many small children, I removed my moon head.

• • •

Kristina said that Greg was pleased by my willingness to humiliate myself for the betterment of his company.

And as I began to feel a bit more confident, I started to throw out more and more creative ideas—some of which were not only praised, they were produced.

Then I decided to push the envelope. Or, shall we say, the feather boa.

Six Flags needed a new TV campaign for a hair-raising new roller coaster. And I had an idea.

"I love it," Kristina responded when I pitched it to her. "I just don't think they'll go for it. It's expensive, and working with a celebrity is always tricky. Let's come up with some other ideas."

We kept brainstorming, but no other concept seemed as perfect.

"Okay," she said finally, "let's present it to the client. If nothing else, they'll appreciate the idea."

"Yay!" I hollered.

"There's only one problem. And I'm really hesitant to say it."

"What?"

"Somebody has to play the role in the presentation. I can't do it. I'm running the meeting. You're gonna have to do it."

• • •

Although Diane and I frequently ate dinner together, that night I begged off. As I sat in my bedroom, alone, I pulled out the Aromatique candle Mother and Dad had given me.

As I lit it, I thought about how far I had come in the past couple of years, discovering my love for writing and an identity I could never have imagined. I knew that selling this campaign would be a feather in my cap and would bring me one step closer to the kind of approval that would make my parents proud. But I was not thrilled with the idea of once again donning drag in order to win approval.

"I've tried to show my creativity," I said quietly to God and whatever angels might be looking after me, "but Greg's not gonna like this."

• • •

I stood outside the conference room, smiling awkwardly at the various Six Flags employees who passed by, as I listened carefully for my cue. I was sweating like a cheap water glass. This moment would either make me or break me.

"Mike, Tom, Greg…" Kristina began, sounding a bit nervous from inside the conference room, "I'd like you to meet the star of your next TV campaign… Phyllis Diller!"

I threw open the door and waltzed into the room wearing a housedress, a fright wig, and a feather boa and carrying a foot-long cigarette holder.

"Ah-hah-hah-*hah*!" I squawked, imitating the famous Diller laugh. "I said I wanted the ride of my life, but *really!*"

The first face I saw was Greg's. His jaw dropped. The blood drained from his face. Steam seemed to be emanating from his ears like a live-action Warner Brothers cartoon.

There was a pause as the men present digested what was happening. A long pause. A pause you could drive a truck through. And then the room exploded in laughter.

"Hey, baby, come sit by me!" one of the Six Flags executives hollered.

"I've got a ride for ya!" his boss yelled.

"Get in line," I replied. "And remember, you have to be this *big* to ride this ride."

More laughter. I glanced over at Greg, who now also began to laugh—uncomfortably. He shielded his face with his hand, as if it were simply too painful to look at me dressed like this.

Kristina and I quickly outlined the TV spots, which would feature Phyllis looking lovely and coiffed as she started the ride, but would finish it a wind-blown, fright-wigged mess.

Everyone turned to the head client.

"How much?"

Kristina gave him a figure.

Another long pause.

"Sold."

A cheer went up from the room. The client winked at me. "And worth every penny."

As we walked to our cars, I was floating on air. Kristina had her arm around me, a proud mother hen parading her chick.

Greg strode up alongside me and smiled. My face lit up. I had not only sold this campaign, I had, it seemed, finally sold him on me.

"So, are you ever gonna bring—what was her name—Kitty around?" There was an odd tone in his voice.

"Oh," I stammered, "um, yeah, soon. It's just—she works a lot on weekends, so I tend to go to Kansas City a lot more than she comes here."

"Uh-huh." We arrived at Kristina's car. He motioned to the feather boa and fright wig I was carrying. "Do you tell her about this stuff?"

"Not really," I said, suddenly deciding that I was probably not supposed to tell my fake girlfriend about my real exploits in gender bending.

"Yeah," he said. "I wouldn't, either."

• • •

I could barely contain my excitement on the day of the Six Flags shoot. Phyllis Diller was the first actual star I had ever met, and I had spent many nights over the past few weeks envisioning thrilling—albeit highly fanciful—outcomes.

She and I would spend hours between takes relaxing in her palatial dressing room, drinking celebrity cocktails and getting massages as she regaled me with stories of old Hollywood. By midafternoon, having bonded over our mutual experiences as outcasts, she would cock her head and say, "You know what, kid? I like you," and by day's end, she would ask me to become her head writer, and I would jet off to Hollywood to write the monologue for her next appearance on Carson.

At 8:00 a.m., it was already eighty-three degrees and humid as Sheree, the account executive, and I waited for Phyllis and her road manager in the portico of their hotel. Sheree had rented a classic Rolls-Royce limousine with a driver to take us all to the theme park, because it would be an arduous shoot day and we wanted our star, who was in her early seventies and thus nearly dead, to be treated in the manner to which she was accustomed.

"Holy *shit!*" Sheree—who was as close to a Junior League prototype as it was possible to get without actually gluing one's jaw shut—shrieked as the limo drove up. The limousine service had not bothered to tell her that, while indeed very 1930s glam, it was actually a town car and roughly the size of a Dodge Dart. It sported a backseat that seated two normal adults or three members of the Lollipop Guild.

At precisely that moment, Phyllis and her manager, Helga, walked out the lobby doors of the hotel. Neither Sheree nor I recognized Phyllis, who had just had another facelift; minus the sequined miniskirt and cigarette holder, she looked like a cross between Joan Collins and Grandma Moses. If Grandma Moses was really surprised.

Phyllis smiled as Sheree introduced herself. She pointed at the car. "What the hell is this? Are you planning to stack us?"

"Oh, n-n-no," Sheree reassured her, stammering as she vamped for time, trying to figure out how to salvage the situation. "Eric, our writer, here," she said, pointing to me, "is driving separately."

I really liked Sheree, but because she was an account executive and, like all AEs, prone to dropping assignments onto my desk at 5:00 p.m. with airy statements like, "Oh, I told the client you'd have some ideas on this by tomorrow," she was automatically the enemy.

"No, I'm not," I replied, smiling beatifically. "I'm outta gas." For a brief moment, it appeared as though Sheree would beat me to death with her pearls.

It was a cramped and sticky ride to the park. The air-conditioning could not keep up with the rapidly increasing outside temperature and humidity, and by the time we arrived,

Phyllis's wig had taken up residence at a forty-five-degree angle, and Sheree's mascara was running down one side of her face. I, however, remained cool as a cucumber, having conveniently elected to ride in the front seat with the driver, where there were vents.

As the shoot day commenced, I quickly realized that this day would not be going quite as I had envisioned. Phyllis, although unusually accommodating for a B-list celebrity of her magnitude, refused to allow anyone into her dressing room. Perhaps it was because she didn't want photo documentation of the eleven pounds of makeup Helga had to apply. Or because her "dressing room" (in Miss Kitty's Saloon) probably wouldn't have passed muster at a Shell station.

She grew more and more cranky as the roller coaster kept malfunctioning and the temperature soared. Finally, in midafternoon, it became obvious that everyone needed a break. A golf cart had been summoned, and Sheree suggested that we take Phyllis on a ride through the park to clear her head.

Sheree rode in front with the driver as I sat in back with Phyllis. As we rolled gracefully through the park, the breeze began to cool us down, and Phyllis, finally comfortable, began to get chatty.

"Thank you for doing this campaign," I said, figuring that "So what's with all the plastic surgery?" might not be my best opener.

"For you, the world," she said smiling and patting my hand. "But never again for thirty-five grand."

"I can't believe I'm sitting here with the first lady of comedy," I said, her warmth reducing me to a puddle of starstruck goo.

"I'll tell ya, sweetheart, there are days when I feel more like the first crypt keeper. I'm too old for this nonsense."

"Are you kidding?" I lied. "You're barely, what, fifty?"

She chuckled. "Blindness becomes you." She smiled at several patrons who pointed excitedly, obviously recognizing her. She leaned forward to the driver. "Step on it."

As we began to head back to the shoot area, we were quiet for a few moments. Then, out of the blue, she leaned over to whisper in my ear.

"You should ask for a raise."

"Oh, thanks," I said, assuming she was referring to the scripts, which Helga had told me Phyllis liked, "but I'm not real popular with the president of the agency."

"That'd be news to him," she replied.

"What?" I said. "Why?"

"We were talking about you this morning. He said he's afraid he's gonna lose you to bigger things."

• • •

In the ensuing days, I began smiling at Greg as we passed in the hallways. He only occasionally smiled back, but now, it didn't matter.

Something had changed.

One day a month later, after the Diller campaign had been completed, he walked into my tiny office and slammed the door. I looked up at him nervously.

"Uh, somebody might need to get a tape out," I said, pointing to the shelves of videotapes.

"They'll wait." He handed me an envelope.

"What's this?" I asked.

"Open it."

What could it be, I wondered? A jury summons? A bill for the Phyllis Diller drag?

Inside was a gift certificate for two nights at a Kansas City luxury hotel, and dinner for two at the restaurant that I had once told Kristina was my favorite there.

My mouth fell open.

"So you and Kitty," he said, "can have a special weekend."

In the moment, I wasn't sure whether this was a dig or a desperate hope that maybe there really *was* a Kitty.

But then, he broke into a smile. And I realized it was a genuine expression of gratitude.

That Friday night, I went to Mother and Dad's for dinner.

"How goes the ad biz?" Dad asked as he sawed corn off a cob with a steak knife to serve to Mother, who refused to touch vegetables without a utensil.

"Much better," I replied. "I think I'm gonna make it after all."

Chapter 12

FREE TO BE YOU AND ME

I had pictured this moment a little differently. Heavyset and dentally challenged, the psychic would be sitting at a card table in a Lane Bryant spring clearance caftan, levitating a Ouija board as it spelled out "PAUL IS DEAD." Her eyes would roll back in her head, flecks of froth appearing at the corners of her mouth as she moaned in a weird voice and shoved a plastic tip jar in front of me.

But Dr. Isabelle was dressed in a power suit and spike heels, and we sat in her chic upper-middle-class living room sipping green tea as she shook her mane of red curls like Glenn Close with a dye job. I was unclear as to what kind of doctor she was, but it appeared to be Doctor of Foxiness.

Until recently, I would have worried that I was going to hell for seeing a fortune-teller. It had long been instilled in me that they were minions of the devil, right up there with Democrats and the Osmonds. But I had long begun to wonder if there was more to God and the universe than what I had been taught in the Baptist church. And given the hellish quandary I found myself in, at this moment advice from any quarter—even an occult one—was welcome.

Yet I was totally unprepared for what this sexy Satanist would say.

• • •

It had all begun when Rudy—my aborted boyfriend Donald's funny friend, with whom I had become closer over the past year—and I had decided to try writing something together. As much as I loved my job at the ad agency, it had been more than two years since I had joined Steckler, and I found myself yearning to write something longer than sixty seconds.

After much deliberation, we had taken a stab at a script for the TV series *The Golden Girls*. It was an obvious choice of show, since Rudy was Blanche Devereaux with a penis and I was Dorothy Zbornak sans the tunics.

Then, unbeknownst to me, via a friend of one of the producers' wives, Rudy managed to get the script into the hands of Christopher Lloyd, one of the show's writer/producers, who was gracious enough to check all the jokes he liked and write encouraging comments, mysteriously stopping short of submitting it for an Emmy.

"Let's do it," Rudy said excitedly when he showed me the marked-up script.

"Do what?"

"Move to LA and become TV writers."

"Oh my God," I said, hyperventilating, "are you serious?"

"I'll find a job at a law firm there, and you can do advertising. That'll tide us over until we can get on a show."

This was a thrilling notion. My head began to fill with visions of a glitzy Hollywood future: Rudy and me buying Porsches that matched our shoes to celebrate landing a seven-figure TV deal; attending galas with Linda Evans and Joan Collins and complaining that they're not as fun as Cagney and Lacey; shopping for homes next to Ann Jillian in the Colony, as we Malibu insiders referred to our exclusive enclave.

"Well," I said hesitantly, "I guess there's nothing really holding us here, huh?"

"Hollywood," Rudy said with bold self-assurance, "is calling. And I for one intend to accept the charges."

• • •

As excited as I was at our decision to move, I was also completely terrified at the prospect of so totally changing my life. But wasn't this what I had always dreamed of? A chance to be creative on a grand scale? A chance to attend high school reunions and drop terms like "the business" and "Bev Hills" while my former torturers blistered with envy?

I was comforted somewhat by the realization that such a move could not be accomplished overnight. I would have plenty of time to get cozy with the idea, since, at best, it would be six months or a year before we could make it to California.

Then Rudy upped the ante. Within six *weeks*, he landed a job at a prestigious LA firm and moved cross-country. And I was now getting daily GlamourGrams.

"I bought a VW Cabriolet convertible. It turns my hair into a fright wig, but it's worth it for the continuous tanning."

"Just got back from shopping at the Polo store on Rodeo Drive. Are you sitting down? I saw Markie Post."

I, on the other hand, was getting nowhere fast. Not a single ad agency had expressed interest in me. Was I not good enough, I wondered? Or was I unconsciously stalling?

Or both?

"How goes the job hunt?"

I heard the usual splashing in the background as Rudy called on his cordless phone from the pool in his apartment building—an annoying habit that he probably thought would serve as motivation, but which only served to make me fantasize about his electrocution.

"Nothing yet," I replied faux confidently as I sat in my newly upgraded office at the ad agency, staring morosely out the window, "but it's only a matter of time."

As more weeks passed, and no LA ad agency responded to my job inquiries, I began to wonder if perhaps Rudy was the only one who was supposed to live a life of LA glamour and television success. Perhaps Rudy was supposed to win an Emmy and live next door to Ann Jillian, and I was supposed to win a free T-shirt from the dry cleaner's and live next door to a crack house. Perhaps Rudy was supposed to become secretly engaged to Tom Cruise, and I was supposed to become secretly engaged to Jack Daniel's. At least, I thought with a dose of pragmatism, that would be an engagement I could probably keep.

Then, one afternoon, Sheree, my account executive, appeared in the doorway of my office, fingering her pearls.

"Greg wants to see you."

These were rarely happy words. While Greg routinely

walked into *our* offices, people who were called into *his* inevitably left with a box of their personal items under their arm and a Mafia-style invitation to burial at sea if they spoke of their time here.

I blanched and began to shake. I was much more secure in my position at Steckler these days. But Greg did not take the prospect of people leaving well. If he had somehow discovered that I was trying to move to LA, maybe he was going to preemptively fire me before I could.

I had told no one. But if Sheree had overheard me cold-calling LA ad agencies and ratted me out, I thought as I marched down the hall, I'm gonna burn down the local Junior League.

I knocked tentatively on the door and stuck my head in.

"Come in," he whispered.

He pointed to a chair in front of his desk as he concluded a phone call, and I sat down nervously. I had only rarely been in his office, and I glanced around at the various awards and photos with St. Louis big shots hanging on his walls, wondering if I would ever be on someone's wall.

He hung up the phone.

"Bet you're a little nervous right now." He sat back in his chair and grinned.

Greg generally only smiled when someone was handing him a check, so this unprecedented exposure of gums to daylight was especially alarming.

"Why would I be nervous?" I replied, my tremulous voice climbing into a range frequented mostly by Steven Tyler.

"Because you should be."

Oh, crap, I thought. *He really does know. He's gonna fire me.*

Of course, why should I be surprised? Holding the bag was not a sport Greg played.

"You see, I expect a lot out of associate creative directors."

The trouble with having only one operative ear was that one could occasionally misunderstand something. Since the days of my first grade school bully, I had always come to assume—usually correctly—that any such words in question were scathingly critical.

"I'm sorry?"

"I'm promoting you to associate creative director. With a $5,000 raise." He leaned forward and extended his hand. "Don't make me sorry I did."

I shook his hand and stood up to leave. "Th-th-thank you," I stuttered, shocked not only at this vote of confidence but at his timing.

I stumbled back to my office in a stupor. What was I supposed to do now? I wanted to take LA by storm, but I couldn't even get an ad agency to return my call. I no longer wanted to live here, but here was a promotion staring me in the face.

And with this raise, I would be able to shop at Oak Tree and buy name-brand pork rinds, maybe even go to the gay bar Nights on evenings when there *wasn't* a drink special. I would be on my way to a new and exciting and successful me.

I would, however, be in St. Louis.

But would this be so bad, I wondered? I had spent my entire life watching the actions of my parents—two people who believed that hard work and ethics, not risk taking, were what earned one kudos. And while it was unclear whether this was innately who they were or because they had two whiny children to raise, those conservative career moves had been my guideline. Who was I to look down on those kinds of life choices now?

Maybe shooting for LA was shooting a little too high.

• • •

As the weeks passed, I began to enjoy my new elevated status at work, my new almost-livable salary, my new mint-green Oak Tree pants that positively screamed *Miami Vice*.

Although my promotion was more in title than in duties, I loved the sense that my creative opinion now mattered more than other people's. And the fact that Greg had promoted me in spite of whatever suspicions he had that I was gay gave me hope for a life and career in St. Louis. Perhaps, as long as I kept who I was quiet, I could become a big fish in this small pond. Sure, it would mean delaying revealing my truth— maybe forever—but it was probably ridiculous to think I could have it *all*.

Of course, staying put meant stalling until I worked up the courage to tell Rudy the truth.

"Any news on a job yet?" Splash, splash.

"Oh, yes," I fibbed, "McCann Erickson is very interested. The pay is absurdly high, but whatever, I can find somewhere to stash the extra money." Screw Rudy and his rooftop pool and his Cabriolet tanning parlor.

"Did you have an interview with McCann Erickson?" he asked a week later.

"No," I replied, "they wanted me to work on New Coke. I mean, I have *standards*."

Rudy would feign understanding at each delay. But I could tell he was losing patience. Especially because, just three years into his law career, he knew that he no longer wanted to be an attorney.

"I can't wait for us to get started writing," he said one afternoon, "because it is *hell* chasing ambulances in four-inch heels."

● ● ●

Just days after my coworker Riley told me about Dr. Isabelle, I arrived at her house for my reading.

She knew nothing about me. And indeed, we had barely exchanged pleasantries before she began furiously jotting things into a notebook as though taking dictation.

"What's happening?" I said nervously. "What are you doing?"

"You're creating a space for yourself to move," she said. "It's a big move. Somewhere with palm trees. Like Florida. No, no, I think it's California."

I was shocked. I had not told Dr. Isabelle anything about my dreams—and fears—about moving. Maybe it was a lucky guess. Maybe people only came to psychics when they were contemplating some kind of big change.

"And they're telling me…"

Who were "they," I wondered as she suddenly began to laugh throatily. The voices in her head who were telling her to kill me?

"Maybe you'll know what this means," she said. "They want you to know that it's time for you to be *you*."

Could that just be something Dr. Isabelle told every client my age, I wondered? A sort of Marlo Thomas *Free to Be… You and Me* moment that filled the space in between what would doubtless be proclamations about the lovely wife and 3.2 children in my future?

Or did something or someone in this room actually know me?

"Well," I said hesitantly, attempting a chuckle, "who else could I be?"

"Apparently," she replied, gazing at me with a funny look, "any number of people." She chuckled. "What are you, *Sybil*?"

I thought about the journey I had begun at the age of sixteen—the search for an identity that would lift me out of the world I inhabited.

"Why have you been trying to be someone you're not?"

"Oh, I guess I'm not always crazy about who I am."

"Well," she said, scribbling away, "time to get over that. 'Cause there are big things ahead of you if you do. But they'll only happen," she said emphatically, "if you move."

I told her about my promotion at work and my conflicted feelings about giving up a sure thing.

"Did I say," she said, leaning forward as her lustrous curls fell around her face, "that it would be easy?"

• • •

For days afterward I contemplated her words, quietly playing the cassette tape of my reading over and over in my bedroom, so that my roommate Diane wouldn't hear. She and Kurt—who had moved back to St. Louis—were my closest friends in the world. But I hadn't had the courage to tell either of them about this dream.

As I sat at work the next day trying to come up with some kind of plan that made sense, Theresa, the agency receptionist, buzzed in.

"It's Kristina."

Kristina, my former boss and longtime cheerleader, had recently left to go to a larger ad agency, paving the way for my promotion.

"Hey, doll," she said from the other end of the phone. "Are you still wearing those freaky contacts?" I had recently gotten colored contacts that made my eyes an attractive shade of demon-possessed blue.

"No," I replied. "People kept asking where I keep the pentagram."

"Hey," she said, "how would you like to be a creative director?"

I nearly dropped the phone. "What are you talking about?"

"Tom Wellington from the Ad Store is looking for a new CD. And I recommended you."

The Ad Store was the hippest ad agency in St. Louis, the kind that created ads that didn't even show the product. The kind that, to promote a new fast food chain, would feature a beaver talking about its period. It was advertising for a new generation, even if the new generation couldn't figure out what the hell the ad was for.

I had just been promoted. And now, someone was potentially offering me yet *another* promotion.

Dr. Isabelle's words rang in my ear. "Big things are ahead of you—but only if you move."

• • •

I set up the Ad Store interview for a date several weeks in the future, telling them that I was under pressure to complete a major campaign at Steckler—giving me time, I hoped, to figure out what to do.

The next afternoon, a few of us gathered in a conference room at the agency to go over demo reels from production companies we were looking to hire for a project. Riley popped in a cassette from Beller and Scheffield, a company in Hollywood whose hilarious radio spots regularly won so many awards you'd think their mothers were voting.

And as the reel began to unspool, so did an idea.

I had only been approaching ad agencies. It hadn't even occurred to me to try a production company. So, the next night, after everyone had gone home, I wrote what I decided was a hilarious fan letter offering my services to Beller and Scheffield. It was a total long shot, given the response rate from LA ad agencies—but what did I have to lose?

A week ticked by. No calls.

Another week.

Nothing.

My interview at the Ad Store was now three days away.

I went home and closed the door to my bedroom and lit the Aromatique Summer Sorbet candle from Mother and Dad. I had moved away from God in the past several years, reeling from what I had been taught was his judgment of who I innately was. But I once again felt a need for some kind of connection, for some sense that there was order to this chaos.

And as I inhaled the luscious, artificial scent of citrus and melon, I began to pray.

"Okay," I whispered, "my future is in your hands."

I waited patiently for some sort of response—a feeling, a spoken word, a nightstand to catch fire.

Nothing.

"Just tell me what the right thing is to do," I said plaintively. "I'm all ear."

No response.

As a young teen, petrified to perform my first trumpet solo in high school Stage Band, I had asked for heavenly guidance—and heard God speak to me. Or so I believed. Granted, I hadn't been his most avid acolyte these past few years, committing an array of sins that would make Jim Bakker look like a choirboy, but I was now endeavoring to reestablish that connection, and in this moment, He seemed entirely disinterested.

• • •

The day before my interview, as I sat in my office wondering what it would be like to be gazing out at the Hollywood Hills instead of a TGI Friday's, Theresa buzzed my phone.

"Ben Scheffield on line four."

"What?!"

"Ben Scheffield. Who is that?" Theresa demanded. She prided herself on being the company clearinghouse for all information that could get you written up or fired.

"Um," I said, thinking fast, "he's an uncle. On my dad's side."

"Well, he's rude. Are all your uncles this rude?"

"No, just the ones who've killed people. Hope you didn't antagonize him."

I glanced heavenward as if awaiting the face of God to appear. Nothing but ceiling tiles with a lot of pencil holes. I took a deeply shallow breath and picked up the phone.

"Hi, Ben," I said brightly, "this is Eric."

There was a loud, elongated sniffing sound on the other end. "This is Clio winner Ben Scheffield," he said. As though the words *Clio winner* (a major advertising award) were part of his birth name. "Of Beller and Scheffield."

I was immediately intimidated.

"Got your letter. Your reel wasn't terrible."

"Thanks," I said tentatively.

"You like writing radio, huh?"

"I love it," I said, clearing my throat and launching into the speech I had prepared should just such an occasion arise. "Radio is theater of the mind, the only medium where you can go from the Alps to Appalachia with just a few sound effects. Where you can create new worlds that don't even exist. Where—"

"Do you have that written on a card?" he said.

"No, a legal pad."

"Well, I guess I should be impressed that you wrote a speech. You didn't even know if I was gonna call."

"Oh, I knew you were gonna call," I replied, summoning every ounce of confidence I could muster.

"Uh-huh," he said. Another long sniff. *Must be allergy season in LA*, I thought to myself. "Your timing is pretty good. We just lost our writer yesterday. He's going to work for the Disney Imagineers, the dumb fuck."

I gasped. Was this coincidence—or divine intervention? Maybe the next question out of his mouth was gonna be, "Would Friday be a good day for us to send the moving van?"

"So, are you moving to LA or something?"

"Uhhhh, well… *yes*," I replied. "Yes, I am." I was astounded at my own bald-faced lie. "I arrive, uh, May 18," I added, picking a random date a couple of months away.

"Well, give me a call when you get here, and maybe we can throw you a freelance project or two."

He sniffled loudly once again and hung up.

I sat there, frozen, the phone still glued to my ear.

I had wanted a job. Any job.

But this one could turn out to be nothing.

Suddenly, Dr. Isabelle's voice rang loudly in my head. "Did I say that it would be easy?"

• • •

From hour to hour, I alternated between elation and panic. Should I stay, or should I go?

I needed advice. From people I trusted. Kurt and Diana, I decided, would know what to do. With an air of mystery that had them wondering if I was about to announce that I had switched back to girls, they gathered for a special dinner the next night.

"You *know* he drives me a little crazy," Diane said as we set the table before Kurt arrived. "He has such a big heart, but he sucks up all the air in the room."

"I know," I said, "but I need his fearlessness tonight. And your unwavering support."

"Unwavering?" she replied, pointing to my head. "Let's talk about that hair."

When Kurt arrived, we sat down to a candlelit dinner at my rustic contemporary dinette set.

"I want to discuss something with you guys," I said as they began to gorge on my elaborately prepared meal of Budget Gourmets and roasted baby Tater Tots. The table had one uneven leg, and I had to keep pressing on one end of it as Kurt—who grew up in a family of all boys and ate like a

Borneo tribesman—kept stabbing his Tater Tots like they might try to escape.

"You do realize," he said, "that this dinner is eating into your runway time."

He and I generally hit the bars three or four nights a week, with Diane in tow on those occasions when I could drag her out, and part of our ritual was my modeling different potential outfits as I blasted Whitney Houston on the stereo and Kurt looked at his watch.

This was one of the many things I would have to give up if I moved, I suddenly thought. Was I really ready to change my life this much?

"Out with it," Diane said, now starting to look concerned.

I took a deep breath and plunged forward. "I got an offer of some freelance work from this production company in Hollywood."

They stared at me, confused at first. Then, slowly, their eyes grew wide. I knew something was wrong when Kurt stopped eating.

I continued. "And I think I should take a chance and move."

I gazed at them, praying for sage words of wisdom and encouragement. They knew how much writing and creativity meant to me.

"To California?" Kurt hollered. "Have you lost your *mind?*"

"Some freelance work?" Diane shrieked. "You can't live on that!"

"Who am I supposed to go to Nights with, then?" Kurt yelled.

"And what am I supposed to do for a roommate?" Diane cried.

"You are bat-shit crazy if you move across the country without a job!"

"You're just gonna throw away everything you've worked for here in St. Louis?"

"Mark my words, you'll be turning tricks within a month."

"Or selling smack."

"But," I said defensively as they paused to suck in air, "Dr. Isabelle said it was meant to be. She said big things awaited me in California."

"Who's Dr. Isabelle?"

"This psychic I went to see."

"You gotta be kidding," Kurt snapped. "You're changing your whole life because of what some freak with a crystal snow globe told you?"

• • •

Later that night, as I lay in bed turning over the events of dinner in my mind, there was a knock on the bedroom door.

"Who is it?" I called out. Like I lived in a boarding house.

"Baby Jane." Diane opened the door. "Can I come in?"

"Sure."

I sat up. The lights were off, but the Aromatique candle was lit.

"It smells like a Caribbean fruit plantation exploded in here." She climbed onto the middle of the bed and wrapped her feet underneath her. I searched her face for clues as to what was going through her mind, finally settling on one of two possibilities:

a) Angry but resigned acceptance; or
b) A plot that involved zip ties, matches, and
a gasoline-soaked rag.

I didn't speak, figuring I'd said more than enough earlier. And she was quiet for a moment as if measuring her words.

"I'm sorry I wasn't very supportive," she finally said. "That just hit me like a ton of bricks."

"Yeah, I can tell," I said, pointing to her face. "You still have a mark. Oh, wait, you've always had that."

"Why didn't you tell me you were at least *thinking* about moving?"

I paused. "I guess I didn't really think it would happen."

It was an unseasonably cold March night, and she pulled the sleeves of her sweatshirt down and shivered a bit. "So, how definite is this, exactly? Should I start looking for a new gay boyfriend?"

"Well," I said, "you can shop around, but no purchases yet." I sighed. "It's an opportunity to really change my life. But it's kind of terrifying."

She gazed into my eyes. "What's so bad about *this* life?"

"Nothing," I said. I grabbed her hands. "You know I adore you. I *love us*. I just… want more."

"More what?"

"I don't know, exactly. Just… more."

"Okay," she said brusquely, yanking her hands away. "Well, I'm sorry I'm not enough for you."

She climbed off the bed and pointed to herself and to me. "I'm sorry *we're* not enough for you."

Tears sprang into my eyes. If I could have married a girl, any girl, it would have been her. Diane had accepted me in a way I had never given Allison the chance to, and it killed me to think that she felt so abandoned.

"Wait!" I cried. "It's not that…" As she headed for the door, I began to panic. "Please don't go!"

She stopped. Hesitantly, she turned and walked back to the bed, her stony expression betraying nothing. Then she grabbed my now-moist face and smiled.

"You deserved that."

• • •

Kurt finally came around, excited about the possibility of a free place to stay in LA. And as much as his and Diane's semiblessings meant to me, I still couldn't pull the trigger. Perhaps it was time, I thought, to go see my sister.

Val, her young son, and her cop husband, Bobby, who could moonlight as a Chippendale dancer since he already had the uniform, lived just a couple of miles from my parents' house. She and I had become closer now that we no longer had the opportunity to throw things at one another from point-blank range.

"I just can't make up my mind," I said plaintively as I bounced my nephew on my lap in her kitchen and she finished lemon oiling the baseboards (since it was, after all, Tuesday). "It could be a great opportunity. Or it could be a disaster. And if I have to come home, they'll have replaced me at Steckler. This could all just come crashing down!"

"God, stop being so dramatic," Val said, her voice muffled

as she crawled along the floor. "If that happens, something else will open up. You're such a control freak."

I heard the pfft of the Lemon Pledge and tried to calm myself by inhaling the delicious lemon scent.

"But let me ask you something," she said. "Why do you have to move two thousand miles away? Couldn't you just move to Chicago? Then you could come home on weekends."

"LA is where the opportunities are for me as a writer. It's where I can become… I don't know. The me I'm supposed to be."

She stood up and threw the rag into the sink, her back to me.

"Yeah," she said—more, it seemed, to herself than me. "It's about time, I guess."

She began to scrub her hands like an emergency room surgeon. "Look," she said matter-of-factly. "You've got talent. I don't. Do you know what it's like to have to listen to you whine about opportunities being handed to you? I'd give my left boob to have your life. Honestly, I don't know what you're waiting for."

"It's scary."

"Sure it is. But you've got Rudy out there. And if you hate it, you can always come back." She carefully wiped the sink dry (insisting, every time she did these things, that she was not Mother) and turned to face me. "I mean, personally, I'm not thrilled about this. I'm losing a free babysitter. But… I think you need to do it."

Our eyes locked. And almost immediately, we both got uncomfortable. We didn't, after all, do emotion.

She turned around again and set a perfectly folded paper

towel under the one glass remaining on the counter.

"So, go," she said quietly. "Be you."

Was she trying to say something else to me? Something larger? I couldn't really be sure.

"Well," I said finally, "if I fail and I have to move back, I'm moving in here."

"That's fine," she replied, brightening. "You know Bobby's always working. We can rent movies and make stuff like we did when we were kids. Don't you miss the potato-chip-and-mayonnaise sandwiches?"

I smiled. Since Mother had never allowed virtually *any* food in the house, our childhood days had been a master class in improvisation. For a moment, I wished we were back in our old basement, dismantling the ceiling in search of boxes of Cheez-Its that Mother had hidden above the ceiling tiles. Life was so much easier then.

"Mother and Dad won't be very happy about it," I said. I'd been agonizing over what their reaction would be. "Don't say anything yet, okay?"

"How can you possibly expect me to keep a secret like this?"

Discretion had never been her specialty. As kids, this was easily resolved with a simple knife fight, or by recording her conversations with her best friend, Vicki, and blackmailing her. Now, it wasn't so simple.

"It's not like I just gave you the nuclear codes," I replied. "Can't you keep your mouth shut for a few days until I work up the nerve?"

"I'll try," she said unconvincingly. "But what's in it for me?"

"I'll name the lead character in my first TV series Val."

"All right," she replied. "But make sure she's hot. And funny."

"Okay."

"I'm thinking Morgan Fairchild with bigger hair."

• • •

Over the next few days, I began to put the first few concrete details into place. And as the possibility started to give way to reality, I knew that the most important and difficult conversation was yet to come.

When I arrived at Mother and Dad's house that weekend, Dad greeted me at the door.

"How's my favorite advertising executive?"

To him and Mother, immediately upon starting at Steckler, I had advanced from new hire to the corner office. Their belief in me was as fervent as their belief in Reverend B. R. Tibbits, which was alternately flattering and disturbing.

I didn't hug Dad. I always wanted to, because he was the kindest man I had ever known, but of course our family avoided physical contact like candy stripers in the leprosy ward.

Mother appeared.

"Come on," she said, smiling. "I defrosted a broccoli casserole. And we got that wine you like that comes in cardboard."

As we sat down to dinner, there was an odd sense of unease in the air. It wasn't the unease of old, the fear that I had done something wrong, that Mother might, at any moment, have a meltdown. The years—or the fact that I could take her in a bar fight—had mellowed her immensely.

This unease, I recognized, was born of the news I carried. Maybe they saw it in my face.

"So you're probably wondering why I wanted to come over."

"Yeah, pretty much," Dad said. "Getting you over here on a Saturday night usually requires cash or a new Tina Turner album."

"I have something to tell you. Something you're not gonna be very happy about."

I cleared my throat and looked at their expectant, anxious faces, and almost immediately realized that, no matter what the consequences, I could not leave St. Louis on a lie. They began to lurch about in their chairs, unconsciously ducking and weaving as though attempting to dodge the words about to emanate from my lips. I took a deep breath to brace myself and finally, forcefully, plunged ahead.

"I'm moving to LA."

There was a loud gasp, followed almost immediately by "Oh, thank God!"

I had not always been the perfect son, failing my parents in many ways (see list, Appendix A). But I had, nonetheless, anticipated a slightly less joyous response—some gnashing of teeth, perhaps, or a simple, "Why, God, why?!!" But to my utter mystification, Mother and Dad began to laugh, as if experiencing some kind of mental or emotional breakdown.

"I got an offer of some freelance work from this production company in Hollywood." I pulled the demo cassette from the production company out of my pocket and set it on the table. "I can't lie to you. It's not a full-time job. But maybe it'll lead to something."

"That's just wonderful!" Mother said.

"Freelance is good," Dad added.

I suddenly realized that they were shell-shocked and simply not dealing with the reality of the situation. I would need to bring them back down to earth. Carefully.

"How much does freelance work pay?" Mother asked.

"I don't know. Maybe not much. Maybe not enough to live on."

"Well, it's California," Mother said. "They pay more for everything out there."

"Yeah," Dad said, "I'm sure it'll be fine."

"I know what you're thinking," I said slowly, as if speaking to a pair of four-year-olds with ADD. "This is really risky. I could fail."

"Oh, nonsense," Dad replied. "You accomplish whatever you put your mind to. Well, except tap dancing. You never did get the hang of that."

"I just feel like I have to try this," I said. "If it doesn't work out, I can always come back, right?"

"Of course," Dad said gently.

"Absolutely," Mother echoed.

There was a long pause as, slowly, their nervous good humor began to fade. The room became very quiet.

I knew what they were thinking. They had always been such careful, diligent people—as parents, as churchgoers, as citizens. They didn't uproot their lives and move two thousand miles on a whim.

Finally, Mother spoke. "You don't want to have regrets," she said softly. "A life of regret is a terrible thing."

"Just promise us you'll come back to visit," Dad said. "A

lot. Okay?"

"I promise," I said, smiling.

"And be careful," he added. "There are a lot of weirdos in California. You don't want to get hooked up with the Hare Krishnas or the Mansons or the Village People."

• • •

I couldn't tell Mother and Dad that I was gay. I knew that I would soon enough, but one life change was enough for today.

Yet I desperately longed to leave with a clean slate. Since my friends at Steckler were throwing me a going-away party, I decided that that would be the perfect venue for some truth telling. (*Mental note, I thought: make up a spreadsheet so I can remember who knows I'm gay and who doesn't.*)

The party was a lovely affair at my art director partner Emma's house, replete with pizza rolls and tears. Kristina came, as did half of the agency, including, surprisingly, an appearance by Greg.

To everyone's relief, he didn't stay long, and as he was preparing to leave, he walked up to me and stuck his hand out. We had shaken hands on a few occasions over the past couple of years, but this time, I noticed an oddly wistful look on his face. He said nothing as we shook, until I began to withdraw my hand and realized he was still holding on.

He just gazed into my eyes for a moment, kind of nodding. Then he looked down and let go of my hand.

"I knew you when," he said simply.

Then he turned and left.

• • •

An hour later, once everyone was properly lubricated and a highly insulting going-away video had been screened, there were calls of "Speech!"

I stood up from the couch and cleared my throat nervously.

"You guys have... you've just been the best coworkers—and friends—anyone could ever want," I said with heartfelt gratitude. "And that's why I feel especially ashamed right now. There's something I have to tell you that I've kept secret for a very long time."

There was a soft gasp as everyone looked at me questioningly.

"I'm gay."

There was a pause, and then Kristina burst into laughter. Slowly, it rippled across the room, building into a wave of knee-slapping, high-fiving hilarity. I stood staring at the group, mystified.

"What is so freaking funny?" I whispered to Kristina.

"Simon saw you going into a gay bar three weeks after you started," she replied, "and he blabbed to everybody."

"Even Greg?" I whispered.

"No," she said wryly, "but after the Rilettes thing, I don't think he needed to."

• • •

Diane had offered to go with me on the road trip to California, and now, on Departure Day, we began to load up my Chevy Cavalier—no mean feat, since we were shoving the contents of my life into a two-door coupe. Diane grunted as she hurled her body against a large box in the backseat.

"Easy there, Butkus," I hollered.

"Once we get into this car," she heaved, "it's gonna take the Jaws of Life to get us out."

"Funny," I replied. I was sweating and stressed and in no mood for comedy.

She handed me an envelope. "Here, open this. It'll be one less thing to cram in here."

"What is it?"

"Your mom sent it to me. She asked me to give it to you when we got to LA, but with all this stuff, I'm afraid I'll lose it before we get there."

Mother sent thank-you cards religiously, and although I couldn't immediately remember what she might be thanking me for, I figured this was another one. I handed it back to Diane as I struggled with a plastic crate of kitchenware.

"Open it and just read it to me, will ya?"

She tore open the envelope and, for a moment, just stood there.

"What?" I said as I battled with the crate, trying to wedge it into a corner of the trunk. "It can't be that personal. It's my mother."

I stopped pounding on the crate long enough to notice a funny look on Diane's face. She passed a typewritten note to me.

This, of course, was not unusual—Mother rarely wrote anything more than her name in cards, usually opting to express her sentiments via an included typewritten note, even in sympathy cards.

I opened the letter.

Dear Eric, it began. *I wanted to share a little story with you. A story I've never told anyone.*

Many years ago, I wrote some chapters of a novel and sent them off to the Harlequin Romance people. They liked them very much, and asked for more.

I was astounded that she had never mentioned this. When, I wondered, did she have time to write them? Between her full-time career and the hours of grout scrubbing, paneling polishing, and dish-towel ironing she did each night, there wasn't much time left for heaving bosoms and willing love grottos.

So, she continued, *I wrote several more chapters, and sent them to them.*

And then, she added, *they rejected me.*

I never wrote again.

I contemplated this life my mother had dreamed of, a life that had never been realized. I wondered if that haunted her.

I don't want you to give up the way I did. Your dad and I know you're nervous about making a go of it in California. But we believe in you. So, we've enclosed a little something to show you how much.

Another piece of paper slipped out of the card and fluttered to the ground. I picked it up. It was a check for ten thousand dollars.

I turned back to the note.

I remember, she concluded, *when you were a teenager, how you often seemed to be pretending to be someone else. I just hope that now, as you start a new life, you know that who you are—this talented, kind, courageous young man—is exactly who you should be.*

So go. Take on the world. Make us proud.

Make yourself proud.

I stood there for a long moment, awash in what-ifs, what could bes, and, for my mother, what had never been.

Finally, Diane put her arm around me.

"You ready? Let's do this thing."

I took a deep breath and nodded. We climbed into the car.

As we both settled into our seats, Diane turned to face me.

"I just want you to know," she said, "I'm still mad at you." She turned to face forward. "But I'm kinda proud, too. I don't think I could do this."

I wasn't entirely sure I could do it, either. But I knew that I had to try.

"So, you, my friend, are gonna be making it up to me for the next four days," she said. "We are going to restaurants that *spin*."

As I pulled away from the lovely, turn-of-the-century brick building we had shared, I gazed up one last time at the dozen tall windows that fronted the street. The warm mid-May sun reflected off the glass, but inside those windows, within the soft beams of mirrored light, I envisioned faces. The faces of the many people I had tried so hard to be.

They smiled, and waved at me.

And I waved back.

···· Acknowledgments ····

To the members of Writers at Work and its creator and mentor, the goddess Terry Wolverton, and the members of my current and beloved writing group, Tiffany Brown, Kathryn Merlo, Charlie Barshaw, and Naz Kutub: You have inspired me, taught me, and been my biggest cheerleaders. You really know how to work a set of pompoms.

To my beautiful and endearingly diplomatic (a quality worth its weight in gold) agent, Kerry D'Agostino at Curtis Brown, who has tirelessly and gracefully shepherded the project and kicked a few sheep when needed.

To the woman with the velvet touch, my editor Hannah Bennett, who gave wonderfully supportive and insightful notes, and made the process a collaborative delight.

To Rosetta's brilliant and hard-working marketing guru, Michelle Weyenberg, who made the most of a tall, gangly guy with one working ear and a desperate desire to be seen.

To Christian Fuenfhausen and Brian Skulnik, whose fantastic cover design and layout totally made the book pop.

And finally, to all of you who buy my books, come to readings, and generally applaud me like the needy child I am… THANK YOU.